My Sister's Keeper

TIMELESS TIPS, TIDBITS & WISDOM FOR WOMEN

Compiled by Amazon Best Selling Author
DR. ANGEL MILLER

Foreword by Dr. Janet L. Newell

Copyright© 2023 Angel Miller Barrino,
Dr. Angel R. Miller,
Angel B. Inspired Inc.

Unless otherwise indicated all scripture references are from the King James Version, New International Version, English Standard Versions of the Bible and a few verses from the Message Bible, used by permission. Scripture quotations are from the ESV® Bible (The Holy Bible, English Standard Version®), copyright © 2001 by Crossway, a publishing ministry of Good News Publishers. Used by permission. All rights reserved.

THE HOLY BIBLE, NEW INTERNATIONAL VERSION® NIV®
Copyright © 1973, 1978, 1984 by International Bible Society®
Used by permission. All rights reserved worldwide.

All rights reserved. No part of this book may be reproduced (except by the co-authors), stored in any electronic system, or transmitted in any form by any means, without written permission from the publisher and primary author, except for the use of brief quotations in reviews. The publisher gives express permission for each author to use their testimonials in reviews, promotions but not to be reproduced in any other publication. Individual author contact information is provided within each chapter.

ISBN: 978-0-69-211641-8

Printed in the USA

Published in the United States by
Angel B. Inspired Inc.
Outer Banks, NC
www.drangelmiller.com
(252) 455-3766

Graphic/Cover Design: Alegna Creates
www.alegnamediasuite.com

TABLE OF CONTENTS

ACKNOWLEDGEMENTS vii
SPECIAL DEDICATION ix
FOREWORD xi
Her Faith, Her Fears, Her Family, Her Feminity,
    Her Finances xv
INTRODUCTION xvii
Experience the Real You and Put Your Best Faith
    Forward 1
A Motherless Child 7
The SHH Anointing 13
Dear Fear 19
Love Is 25
Ministering on Broken Pieces 33
Just Breathe: Enhancing Your Life by Resting in God 39
Credit Check: Tips for Turning Your Credit Zero
    Into a Credit Hero 45
Finding Me 55
Remember Me 63
Crumbs, the Remix 67
Mirror, Mirror 73
Winning at Wealth 83
Bonus Stuff & Inspiration 91
THE CONCLUSION OF IT ALL 103
ABOUT DR. ANGEL MILLER 119
REFERENCES 123

"Who can find a virtuous woman? for her price is far above rubies. The heart of her husband doth trust safely in her, so that he shall have no need of spoil. She will do him good and not evil all the days of her life."

~Proverbs 31:10-12

ACKNOWLEDGMENTS

To my mother: Katherine Ann Miller - The first woman to love me, to make me feel safe; the woman who first believed in my dreams and aspirations, who gave me hope that I could achieve most anything I set my heart and mind to.

To my dad: thanks for being a great father and instilling values, respect, and dignity. For teaching me to live humbly and righteously.

To my brothers & all the males in my life who respect women—thank you!

To my daughter Janae Necole Sharpe: My number one fan. "Guess How Much I love You?"

To my sisters: Danielle Y. Miller & Karen D. Miller
"*We Dem Miller-Gilmer Girls*"
I love you both. Thanks for being there.

Special thanks to my Aunt Jenny Boyd for always being present in my life, for loving and supporting me since birth.

To all my aunts & uncles who have supported and provided wise counsel, thank you!

To my closest friends: Thank you for our Sisterhood and bond; a few decades of moments I cherish for the love and friendship we share. For your daily prayers, text messages, phone calls, "ah ha" moments and more, I am truly grateful.

To my nieces: Aerial Monae Johnson and Lamiya U. Miller—
Keep blossoming and moving into your destiny.
I love you both.

To my female cousins: I am grateful for being able to grow with you. Thank you for being an important part of my life. We have grown up together.

To My Spiritual Mom & Apostle: Dr. Janet Newell,
Thanks for supporting me, believing in Most High's purpose for me and for the spiritual pep talks.

"Special Acknowledgement"
Dr. Richard Martin – Thank you for your professional guidance and clinical urging to complete this book. Our weekly meetings of clinical supervision, "life interruptions," and support have been instrumental in the acceleration of my professional growth and personal development as a therapist and an individual. You are a tremendous blessing and answer to prayer.

To EVERY WOMAN who has made a difference or left an indelible mark on my heart— I love you!
This is for each of you.

SPECIAL DEDICATION

This book is dedicated to the women who paved the way for me, who are no longer with me. The women who taught me grace, class, business savvy, cleaning, cooking, and all sorts of life lessons—hard lessons, love lessons mixed with wisdom and truth serum. These are the women who helped guide my journey, shape my perspective, wipe my tears, and nurture my wounds. These are the women who, through their own experiences, joined my parents in the task of teaching me how to live and learn God's will for me. For this, I am eternally grateful and honored to have had them in my world.

My grandmothers
Elizabeth Della Gilmer and Louise J. Miller

My aunts
Mary Minor, Mary Hazel Bass, Martha Miller,
Geraldine Moore, Clementine Jones

My Mother in Love
Mollie Bettie Sharpe

My "Other Mother"
Helen S. Mahoney

Two of my dearest friends, who are no longer with us:
Michelle Williams & Lawana L. Best

FOREWORD

Being a woman in today's world is very difficult. Being a Woman of Yah gives us more of an advantage to overcome the vices and hiccups of society's views regarding the perfect woman. The hardest part of coming into your own is overcoming who you are not. The baggage of abusive words, relationships and situations will eventually make us strong; however, it is the healing process that we must endure in order to get to places of strength and maturity.

The Bible tells us that the older women are to teach the younger women. Yet what happens when the older women need healing as much as the younger women? Being our Sister's Keeper is an honorable placement in Yah; bringing accountability and growth in the lives of women of all ages—especially those who Yah has mandated to bring healthy productivity in the earth.

Whether you are a Spiritual Mother, Mentor, Spiritual Daughter or Mentee accountability and encouragement is so vital to the growth of a woman who has Yah given purpose.

This book, *My Sister's Keeper*, is designed to be all of that. When one reads this book, they will be given hope and encouragement. This book provokes our sisters not to give up but to grow up.

My Sister's Keeper is a blessing for The Women of Yah.

>   —*Dr. Janet L. Newell, PhD.BC D.Hu, D.Clc. MCC, BCA*
>   *Gathering At Yeshiva Worship*
>   *Yeshiva Worship International Fellowship World Span*
>   *Rehoboth International Bible College*

PHENOMENAL WOMAN
Maya Angelou

Pretty women wonder where my secret lies.
I'm not cute or built to suit a fashion model's size
But when I start to tell them,
They think I'm telling lies.
I say,
It's in the reach of my arms,
The span of my hips,
The stride of my step,
The curl of my lips.
I'm a woman
Phenomenally.
Phenomenal woman,
That's me.

I walk into a room
Just as cool as you please,
And to a man,
The fellows stand or
Fall down on their knees.
Then they swarm around me,
A hive of honey bees.
I say,
It's the fire in my eyes,
And the flash of my teeth,
The swing in my waist,
And the joy in my feet.
I'm a woman
Phenomenally.

Phenomenal woman,
That's me.

Men themselves have wondered
What they see in me.
They try so much
But they can't touch
My inner mystery.
When I try to show them,
They say they still can't see.
I say,
It's in the arch of my back,
The sun of my smile,
The ride of my breasts,
The grace of my style.
I'm a woman
Phenomenally.
Phenomenal woman,
That's me.

Now you understand
Just why my head's not bowed.
I don't shout or jump about
Or have to talk real loud.
When you see me passing,
It ought to make you proud.
I say,
It's in the click of my heels,
The bend of my hair,
the palm of my hand,
The need for my care.
'Cause I'm a woman
Phenomenally.
Phenomenal woman,
That's me.

Maya Angelou, "Phenomenal Woman" from And Still I Rise. Copyright © 1978 by Maya Angelou. Used by permission of Random House, an imprint and division of Penguin Random House LLC. All rights reserved. Source: The Complete Collected Poems of Maya Angelou (Random House Inc., 1994)

*Her Faith, Her Fears,
Her Family, Her Feminity,
Her Finances*

INTRODUCTION

My Sister's Keeper began as a collaboration project focused on sharing tips, tidbits, and words of wisdom for women from all walks of life. Since then, this project has had many twists and turns, and the journey has been tedious. Through my own personal health and family issues, concerns from the contributors, being unable to secure the design team and other obstacles, this project has now become a full-blown collaboration featuring eleven contributing authors and myself, includes a bonus section for recipes, original quotes, and inspirational anecdotes from a few members of my close network, including my sister. The platform has grown to encompass stories addressing every aspect of a woman's existence: *Her Faith, Her Finances, Her Fears, Her Confidence, Her Future*, and much more. There are snippets of financial tips; recommendations on how to overcome feelings of doubt, low self-worth, body image issues, anxiety, depression. We discuss single mom woes, marriage and relationship ills, physical fitness and self-care as musts. This book shares a bit of everything, but not everything. Women make the world a better place. We are stronger than strong, capable of accomplishing numerous things at once.

This book invites women to begin a new journey of wholeness, embrace the SISTERHOOD, and find solutions to life's daily challenges.

As I began researching for this book, I realized that *"My Sister's Keeper"* is a common sentiment among women around the globe. This book is intended for your average, everyday woman to share her wisdom, "experience, strength, and hope" with other everyday women. There's a young mom, single and fighting daily to ensure the safety and quality of life for her children ... This is for her. There's a business woman working multiple jobs to create enough capital to "get her business, ministry or non-profit off the ground" ... This is for her. There's a woman who has experienced multiple traumatic events, maybe struggling with her confidence & self-esteem... This is for her. *My Sister's Keeper* is for me, you, and every other woman out there who has been through something or currently living something. This book is intended to provide insight, joy, encouragement, and guidance through life's moments.

As I considered my own experiences, I acknowledge that I have not always been "a sister's keeper." In my younger years, I made numerous mistakes, lacked guidance, and had significant emotional issues to navigate. However, Most High taught and healed me, through His unconditional and unfailing love and His Spirit. He sent older women to teach, strengthen and empower me; therefore, I can share the same wisdom imparted to me. Galatians 5:22-23 reads, "But the fruit of the Spirit is love, joy, peace, forbearance, kindness, goodness, faithfulness, gentleness, and self-control. Against such things there is no law." Living according to this scripture and many others has saved my life and placed me in a better position to help women grow and excel.

This book is for you ... woman of Yah, woman of purpose, woman of stature, woman of wealth, woman of faith, woman of integrity, woman of hope. We are your sisters, we are your keepers!

~ Dr. Angel Miller & MSK Contributors

EXPERIENCE THE REAL YOU AND PUT YOUR BEST FAITH FORWARD

Minister Karen Moore

Life is such an amazing experience, a journey with many twists and turns. You were created to make a difference in this world and that will not come easy. Experiencing the true person that God created you to be will create an experience like none other. Being intentional about clarity on your purpose is a must. Intentional is defined as done on purpose; deliberate. Putting your best faith forward is going to require you to be deliberate and purposeful in everything you do. I believe that having great faith is the beginning of being intentional. Allow me to share with you the three ways to experience the real you intentionally by putting your best faith forward.

First, let's discuss being intentional. What does it mean for you to be intentional? I am so glad you asked. The definition of intentional is done on purpose; deliberate. You must be deliberate about achieving any goal you set out to achieve. I have discovered that being intentional requires a shift in your mindset. When you are truly ready to be intentional, the urgency of it all will play a great part in shifting your mindset. Every action, thought, and decision begins in the mind. Recently, I began the journey to being healthier and taking better care of my health and being active. Now, I've done this before, but now I wanted to be intentional about it being a way of life and not something I stop doing at the drop of a dime. When I shifted my mindset and decided to make a change, I became more disciplined. Once you shift your mindset in your situation, it is necessary to lay out a plan filled with action steps to help you reach your goal. Allow me to interject that you do not have to complete all action steps to your goal immediately. If you attempt to do everything at once, you will become overwhelmed, frustrated and you will quit. I know this path all too well. My healthy journey began with me at least two miles daily, beginning every morning at 5:45 am at least 5 days a week. Becoming intentional also brought along discipline. You may begin your journey to purpose and find yourself battling in your mind about your previous track record of failing quitting before. Know that the enemy will use the same tricks to try and break you down. Don't fall for it! Continue being intentional in your quest for better and you will experience it. Now, that you have become intentional it's time to build the faith to keep going.

Got faith? Hebrews 11:1 (NLT) says, "Faith shows the reality of what we hope for; it is the evidence of things we cannot see. So, faith is hope with no evidence that it will even take place, but we still believe it will. Faith is built by spending time in the word of God, which will fill you with truth and knowledge to sustain you. I like to call it "now faith." Now faith, in my definition, means that we believe God and that He is more than able to do whatever we ask in faith, suddenly.

All you need is faith the size of a mustard seed. When that small amount of faith is established, we then have enough to build upon. Faith is not faith until it is tested and tried. Just like a diamond must go through extreme pressure before it comes out a beautiful gem, so do we. Each obstacle and situation that we face and get through, strengthens our faith. The pressure pushes out the impurities and creates strength (a gem) like none other. Each time your faith is strengthened you can attack anything in your life with a stronger faith and with great confidence. Faith is why we continue to move forward in what our assignment is here on earth, because we know that God created us with purpose in mind and having faith in Him will propel us forward into our destiny. It's now time to move forward.

Moving forward intentionally in faith is so powerful. Building a strong faith intentionally will propel you into the more that God has for you. We spend a lot of time scratching the surface, falling into a pattern of doing what others are doing and never getting into what God has for us. But since you are now intentional with your now faith, you are headed to your purpose!! In the process of building intentionality and faith, you are uncovering the amazing visions, dreams and ministries God planted inside you when He created you. What you possess is needed. The care taken in our creation is unmatched. There is nothing we possess from creation that was a mistake and is not needed. I spent years searching for my purpose. I even asked God, "What is my purpose?" I was so lost, spiritually. But when we ask God a question, be prepared for the answer. I went on a quest and found out what my purpose was, and life changed. When you find your purpose, you will know it. You will be connected spiritually, and things will begin to take place that you once thought may not be for you. Again, God makes no mistakes and has equipped you and I with all we need to build His kingdom. This is your time to keep stepping out, putting your best foot forward in faith, intentionally.

Life is an experience that you can enjoy when you're in a position to prosper in purpose. The building of your faith intentionally prepares you for this experience. Whatever it is you were created to be and achieve in this earth, for the kingdom, having strong faith is a pre-requisite to achieve it. I am on a mission to be healthier, lose weight and experience all the benefits that come with achieving this goal. To achieve this goal, I first must address the issue and shift my mindset.

Understanding our weaknesses and triggers is going to help us combat all distractions, disruptions and situations that come to halt purpose growth. Continue seeking God for each step in your journey. The definition of insanity is doing the same thing and expecting different results. The God-connection will order your steps and you will walk the path created for you. And even on our life's journey, we will encounter obstacles that may bruise us or throw us down to our knees. But the excellent thing about giving our best to God is that He will always be there to care for our scrapes and bruises and help us up each time we fall. Even when it's our own fault. This journey requires strong faith to push past what has always been done to achieve what you must do in order to be successful.

You are now experiencing the real you! The woman that God created you to be in the first place. Now, you can feel the connection even more because you are intentional in your faith to build upon what God has given you. Walk in purpose and power with intentional faith. Sit daily with God, seek His detailed instructions, and listen to His plans for you. Enjoy your life experience in God and keep walking, putting your best faith forward!

Minister Karen Moore is a wife, mother, author, and empowerment coach/speaker. Karen is enjoying life with her wonderful and loving husband of over 16 years, Cornell Moore. They are very proud parents of two daughters, Brianna and Kennedy.

As owner of EmpowerYou Apparel, EmpowerYou Bling Accessories and the visionary and founder of Words Work Wonders with KarenB.Moore.org, Karen uses her multiple platforms to motivate, educate, and encourage many people in different stages of their life and empowers others to live their best life from the inside out. Karen B. Moore is a woman created to shake YOU up and provide confidence and empowerment for the purpose of helping women see their true passion, which leads them to their true purpose! To stay in touch with Karen Moore or invite her for events, please email karen@karenbmoore.org. She can also be found on Facebook: @karenmoore as well as on Instagram: @karenbmooreorg. Don't forget to follow the Hashtag #EmpoweringYouFromThe InsideOut

A MOTHERLESS CHILD

Minister Tracy Eleazer

On November 29, 2015, my life forever changed. Before this date, my mother found a lump on her left breast; it was Thanksgiving Day 2014. She let me feel the lump, I was shocked and didn't know how to react. As time passed, she was finally seen by her primary doctor, different tests were done, including a biopsy, X-rays, and blood work. She was diagnosed with Stage 4 Metastatic Breast Cancer. Once my mother heard the words "Stage 4 Breast Cancer," I believe she felt numb; she didn't hear anything else that was said to her. A few doctors came in and out of the room, scheduling different appointments for her and providing various options for treatments. During a quiet moment, with just the two of us, she cried. As I sat there in complete silence, I was unable to move and felt trapped. I was astonished by the information I was being presented with, and the sight of my mother in such disarray was overwhelming.

The Oncologist came in to advise that her cancer must be treated aggressively, and treatment needed to begin soon. She began her 1st treatment on 8/4/2015. Naturally, she was scared and nervous. That day, while we sat on the bench waiting for valet parking, she said, "I don't know what that lady is looking at me for, looking at me like I am crazy." As I lifted my head to see what she was fussing about, I noticed my mom was smoking a cigarette. I said, "Ma, why are you smoking a cigarette sitting here right in front of the cancer center? Half of these people have cancer from smoking, and you are sitting here smoking?" She replied, "I know. I am just nervous, that's all. I said, "Ma, can you wait until we get in the car or at home?" But thinking back on that moment, I realize how she must have felt. We laughed about it once she got home.

She continued with the treatments for a few weeks, the doctors had advised that the chemotherapy was working, and that the tumor was shrinking. We were so hopeful that she was going to be okay. My mom wanted to hear that the cancer was gone. We continued praying to God; trusting and believing Him for healing, for a miracle to take place in her life.

Even though my mom began treatments in August, her health began to change in October; she became sick. She was in and out of the hospital and developed pneumonia. She was admitted to ICU and was sick with different things happening at once. After conducting additional tests, doctors determined that the cancer had spread to her brain, necessitating the administration of additional chemotherapy instead of radiation treatment, which was not considered safe for the brain. More time had passed as she was unable to walk or hold things in her hands, she was frail. Once more tests were taken, it was determined that the cancer had also spread to her bones, and she was experiencing a lot of pain. I would spend the night with her whether she was in the hospital or at home. Whenever she was at home, I would sleep in the bed with her. As my mom's only child, I was also her sole caregiver.

Sadly, my mom's health deteriorated quickly, and Hospice provided some of her care. Since I worked from home, I decided to bring my mother home to live with me. This worked best, allowing me to take care of her and preventing her from being alone at the hospice facility. The doctors hoped that she would live through the holidays, but of course, they were unsure.

During the time my mom was at my home she was alert, able to talk, and understand things. In my heart, I felt that she needed to give her life to Christ Jesus. As family and friends visited her, I updated them regarding the status of the cancer. We prayed, and my mom cried. One of the ministers that was present offered Christ Jesus to my mom, and she accepted Christ as her Lord and personal savior. A few days passed; she lived through Thanksgiving. She slept but did not respond as normal; noticing that she began refusing pain medications. I contacted Hospice to let them know that she was doing a lot of sleeping and not really responding to me. At the time, I was advised to keep a watch over her, and they would send a nurse over whenever one was available to come out and assess her. I eventually had to call the ambulance because things started changing for her, she was rushed to the hospital with a DNR in order, which broke my heart. Once the doctors assessed her, it was determined that she was at the end of her life.

Having accepted what God had allowed, I decided to let her rest. As we all sat at her bedside watching her transition, I talked to her and told her I loved her, and played worship music for her. I even played her favorite song 'God Is Trying To Tell You Something from the Color Purple movie – the last song she heard before taking her last breath and died on November 29, 2015, at 8:48pm.

At that moment, I knew it was God who gave me the strength to hold myself together and not become emotional. At that moment, I felt I had to be strong and supportive for my children and for my granddaughter, who my mother loved so dearly. Many times, the pain of losing my mother is unbearable; the grief makes my body ache as if having the Flu. Some days I do well, and I do not cry, but other days, not as much.

Unfortunately, my mother was not fully part of my life when I was younger, however, when we reconnected, we became inseparable. I never resented her for not being in my life; I just wanted her and to spend time with her. God kept us through it all, until she passed. There is hope, and I don't cry as much I used to, I feel like God is healing me. I know that I will never stop missing and crying, especially on special days. I am her only child; this grief is something that I have to bear alone. Not only that, but I honor her all the time, I miss her, If I had one wish that would be for her to come back into my life again so we can reconnect once more.

Minister Tracy R. Eleazer is a native of Greensboro, North Carolina. She is a mother of three (Diesha, Nadia, and Yuquan) and a grandmother of eight and four bonus grandchildren. She is the CEO of *Creations by "Tracy"* founded in January 14, 2013. Tracy enjoys writing fiction books that provide details of personal events which have occurred in her life. Her first book is titled, *God, My Mom & I.*

THE SHH ANOINTING

Pastor BJ Relefourd

The submission request and the subject matter arrived unexpectedly. Subsequently the topic was of such relevant nature. I knew this was not only a call to attention, but a call to submission. This clarion call descended upon me to share a phrase and the definition or the phrase I was currently filing an application to register and trademark.

The phrase holds such a presence in my life. I wholeheartedly believe it would be beneficial to those who are on a journey of growth and development. As stated in the book, *The Lady is a Leader*, a monumental principle is that, everything is not profitable to say.

A lady should learn in the primary stages of a journey of excellence that volume does not dictate the level of leadership. The quality of words spoken far exceeds the quantity of words spoken. This is the point where the phrase is implemented and should be used in an effort to maintain excellence in monologue and courtesy in dialogue.

The phrase to which I am referring to is, "*Get a Shhh Anointing*". Had I embraced this concept much earlier, I could have eliminated much of the turmoil l experienced, due to the lack of discipline of speech. As the passage of scripture states in Titus the second chapter, the older women should teach the younger women. The grace of maturity was also recognized by a former producer at WATC -TV 57 which teamed two great women of maturity and grace, along with myself and proclaimed us as *Sisters with Class*, which became a periodic segment on the Christian Television Network.

The Shhh Anointing relies on the ability to refrain from interjecting commentary when it is unnecessarily warranted. Every comment does not require commentary. The capability to engage in a setting and not comment unless there is a release from the Holy Spirit is critical to maturity. In some situations, maturity of tongue allows you to let someone else answer the question; even though you know the answer. Your relinquishing to answer a question may build the confidence of someone who may be a victim of low self-esteem or lack of confidence.

The Shhh Anointing also allows the liberty to listen with clarity to what is being said and most importantly to what is not being said. Continuance of conversation causes a combustive traffic jam of thoughts, emotions, and conflict of resonating opinions. *The Shhh Anointing* will dismiss the onset of statements of insinuating comments, which fill the environment with negative connotation.

The Shhh Anointing

The Shhh Anointing is also an enormous learning tool. Much information has been obtained by being quiet and listening attentively and only responding if required or requested. Secondly your inadequate knowledge of a particular subject will remain concealed. The lack of experience, maturity or insensitivity to the subject being discussed will never be revealed if *The Shhh Anointing* is applied.

The anointing in this application can be explained is the supernatural crushing of the oil, upon your natural will to respond. Commonly it's a normal exercise to engage and interject phrases thoughts and opinions. More often than not, thinking before releasing a complete paragraph is not something which is considered or contemplated prior to statements or opinions. Unfortunately, once a comment is released, an apology may quickly follow, however the damage has been inflicted. Contrary to the old adage, "sticks and stones break bones and words never hurt". We've learned over the years this statement has been found to be untrue and highly contradictive.

Formulating a consciously positive speech initiative before actually making a comment or issuing an opinion has proven critical to the positive results of a constructive and meaningful conversation.

Literally, many misconceptions and misinformed logics have derived from misunderstandings, and not well thought out gestures of comment.

Asking the Holy Spirit for guidance before uttering a word has proven fruitful and beneficial to the correct input as well as the correct timing of the input.

Timing is another component of the Shhh Anointing. Implementing the skill of knowing the rhythm of when to interject, and when to remain quiet; alert but quiet.

The Shhh Anointing will provide you with the accurate signal which alerts you when it is your turn to enter the conversation. Timing coupled with tone if not asserted properly can derail a well-planned board meeting or derail the most thought out negotiations.

Surely, you would not want to be the cause of an abrupt end to what could have been one of, if not the most epic affair in history.

Let's address tone. The tone of any given statement or comment is crucial to the manner it is delivered. You may have meant to deliver a strategic comment in a particular manner, however because you didn't make a conscious effort to think before you spoke, the recipient received your statement with a negative connotation.

Furthermore, consider to whom you are speaking, a particular phrase or form of humor may be embraced or welcomed in one particular group. The phrase or humor may present itself as offensive or un welcomed or even tolerated in another. It's always wise to research the demographics of your audience. Whether the audience is an audience of one or an audience of 100 or more. Exercising quality speech patterns surpass implementing a multi-syllable exchange which may leave the recipient searching for an accurate response.

Expressing common pleasantries are welcomed multi-culturally and do not normally imply the need for apologies or well-meaning regrets.

The Shhh Anointing is a valuable and viable component. It is idealistic that an adolescent, a millennial, an aspiring leader as well as a seasoned individual receive, and digest a healthy dose of *The Shhh Anointing*; it is a much-needed accessory, when worn properly. This posture transcends seasons, cultures, ethnicities and denominations. It is quite fortunate this submission arrived in ample time to allow some flexibility as related to creating positive speech patterns and releasing some of the old language models which has proven to be harmful and not conducive to a positive dialogue environment.

Dr. BJ Relefourd is a submitted daughter of the Father and wife to the incredible love of her Life, Reverend Marion Relefourd for over 43 years. She's been recognized as a trailblazer, a woman of God who operates in lightning years ahead of her time. Dr BJ, along with her husband are the founders of *Vision of Life Ministries* and *Vision of Life Ministries E-Church* Campus. Dr. BJ is also the founder and Visionary of the *Women of Power Network*, which includes the *Lady Leader Blog* and Academy. Additionally, she is a certified Life Coach and presently hosts *The Vision Speaks* with her husband. Together they present episodes of *The Word and Worship* and *The Vision Speaks2* which includes practical biblical and ministry episodes, with sound scriptural teachings. A Kingdom Authority Media Producer, Dr. BJ is known as the *Lady Leader who Walks in Power*. If you are ever privileged to see the comedic side of her, you will be richly blessed. Her first ministry is to God, her husband, and her family. You may find her on social media as Dr. BJ Relefourd.

DEAR FEAR

Lady Dawn Runyon

Dear Fear,

I'm writing to let you know that I have finally made the decision, after what seems an eternity, that I can NOT and will NO LONGER tolerate living controlled by you!

I know that after living together for so long, this may be hard for you to grasp, and I'm sure you probably even doubt my ability to do so, but I am DONE. Furthermore, I'm done believing the lies that have convinced me that I'm not competent, capable, or worthy of having the life that I desire to live. Your demands and doubts have kept me small – kept me stuck, holding on to compromise and anxiety, worried that my expectations and dreams would leave me broken and ashamed. I realize now what has broken me and made me ashamed more has been looking back and seeing all the amazing things I didn't do because I listened to you.

In the beginning, I thought that some of your mind games protected me, giving me pause to really take time to count the cost and make a thorough decision. However, over time your overbearing presence and your true nature became stifling, debilitating, and left me paralyzed; unable to make the simplest of decisions and watching life pass me by while others accomplished the goals and achievements that I once felt destined to achieve.

Fear, you have lied, stolen, and destroyed so much, yet, I have met someone who not only promises, but has shown himself to be trustworthy and more than capable of giving me back EVERYTHING! He has done it for others, and I know in my heart that He will do the same for me. When I spend time with Him, I find my wildest dreams within reach – I have focus, clarity, and courage. Not only can I see myself achieving my goals and dreams, but with Him, I can trust that the steps I must take and the doors that I need to open will be provided. In all the years I spent with you, I've never felt this FREE, the fog has lifted, and the "son" is truly shining on me.

I do want to thank you, though; because of your disappointing and suffocating ways, I can now recognize what it feels like to experience hope and joy. I am confident that when I sense any trepidation or confusion that it is my "alarm" to dig in deeper and lean even more on Jesus. Oh, that's His name by the way, Jesus – doesn't it just make you shudder?

No longer yours,
ME

Sister, like a controlling, gas-lighting, abusive partner, fear wants to keep you small, insecure, and doubting your true power and worth.

Hear me, YOU are ONLY limited by your OWN FEAR and YOUR INACTION! However, we often give 'fear' too much power and control in our lives – to our own detriment. Everything that you desire to do, is only a matter of DECIDING to do it. Win or lose, you won't ever know what you are fully capable of until you try. I get it, it seems too easy or simple to say "just do it" (Nike, Inc. 1988) – but that little shoe company wouldn't be as successful as it is if their slogan didn't prove true after all these years.

After all, you can't judge whether something is a success or failure until you DO it – like the old saying goes, "the proof of the pudding is in the eating." But, oh how fear will make us quit before we even begin.

There is a mnemonic for FEAR that clearly lays out why it holds such power over many – *False Evidence Appearing Real*. It's generally believed by psychologists and scholars of "worry" that up to ninety percent of the things we worry about never come to pass, and the 10% of the time it does, it usually isn't as devastating as we tell ourselves it will be, as noted in *The Worry Cure* by Dr. Robert L. Leahy. That dread of the impending harm, rejection, and ridicule you feel, while valid, is FALSE – what evidence is there that it will happen? That you will meet the fate that has caused you to not act? Because it has happened to others, or maybe even to you in the past, doesn't mean it will happen now and even IF it has, you SURVIVED IT! On the flip side, how often do you look back and realize that it wouldn't have been so bad or that you could have done it after all?

Don't get me wrong, there is a healthy level of fear. Healthy fear alerts you to dangers and makes you aware of situations or people that may not be safe for your survival. When it shows up, it challenges your thinking by causing you to discern your thoughts: *Why should I do "A" or why do I want "B"? What is the worst thing that COULD happen if I do this…or maybe, what is the best thing that could happen?* A healthy perspective of fear might also prompt you to seek the advice and wise counsel of someone in a position to objectively weigh your options without the emotionally charged attachment that we often have to our own decisions. That's why having a coach or mentor is so impactful. Unhealthy fear does just the opposite. It convinces you that if you need to ask for help or guidance, then you must be incompetent – it condemns and shames you. Watch any biopic or read an article discussing any number of successful individuals and you'll likely hear them credit a mentor or coach in helping them overcome that internal battle of fear.

Having someone who is able to help you come to your own best decisions, who will support and encourage you to go after your dreams, is a huge key to success.

Proverbs 15:22 says "plans fail for lack of counsel, but with many advisers they succeed." Whether you are a believer in the word or not, if you find yourself stuck, not starting that business you've dreamed of for so long; not publishing that book you've been working on for years; still talking yourself out of going back to college; continuing in a toxic relationship because you think you won't find anyone better; worried what your friends or family will think, say, or do…and so on, I urge you to accept this teaching and surround yourself with individuals that you can entrust your fears to, and seek advice to demolish fear's stronghold in your life.

WARNING: Don't seek advice from your girlfriend who hasn't ever left a 20-mile radius from her home, okurrr! (In my Cardi B voice.)

Obviously, I'm being facetious. However, be wise in seeking input from others. Our friends and family can often project their own fear onto us in an attempt to shield us from disappointment and failure. To move past your fears, choose someone that will actually challenge you, but will also remind you about the strength and power you have within!

Sister, if you didn't hear me the first time, let me say it again – "You are ONLY limited by your own FEAR and IN-ACTION!" Taking more time to 'get ready' won't solve the issue. How much time, energy, and money have you wasted to this point, and what do you have to show for it? Fear is a paralyzer. Left unchecked it will kill, steal, and destroy your dreams, aspirations, and future. Can't you see that evidence in your life? Is your present state the result you see when you visualize your success? Have you achieved what your heart has ached for all these years?

There is nothing outside you preventing you from what you DECIDE to do, the barrier is internal. It's time that you end this unhealthy relationship with fear and begin to experience and enjoy the beauty of your God given potential and passions. I write this as much for myself as I do for you – Sister, you got this, now go get your blessing!

LOVE IS

Lady Dawn Runyon

As a teen and even a young adult I wanted to be loved, but I had no clue what LOVE was. I thought it was all about feeling wanted and belonging to someone, so I desperately wanted to be claimed, to be someone's Girlfriend, ole' Lady, BAE, or Wifey. I would have given just about anything to have some man put a label on me (and DID!). Without that distinction I often felt illegitimate, inadequate, unworthy, and unwanted. So, when *he* showed up looking all sexy in those green Army fatigues and offered to put his "label" on me, asking to marry me, I just KNEW this was my chance to really be loved – I was WRONG!

There is an old axiom that says, "what you don't know can't hurt you" but that is one of the biggest LIES of ALL time. Whether it's not knowing your significant other is cheating on you, or that the man you call your father really isn't your father, to not knowing that the medicine (drug) you are taking is laced with some poison, NOT knowing the truth can be very harmful (mentally, emotionally, and physically) and, in some instances, it can be FATAL. The bible, in its wisdom says just that – in Hosea 4:6, it reads *"my people perish for lack of knowledge"*. Nowhere is that more relevant than in relationships. What I didn't know about healthy and unhealthy relationships I was fortunate to learn after naively suffering through many abusive and toxic relationships – LOVE SHOULD NOT HURT!

Unfortunately, many of us find out too late that we don't know what we don't know. When it comes to dating and choosing life partners, like me, many people seek after things and people outside of themselves to define their identity, their worth, and their fulfillment. Not being taught by healthy, whole, and safe individuals how to have a loving relationship with someone else, or for that matter, how to love one's own self, has damaged many individuals and families. Because falling in love happens so organically, we fail to realize that there are levels to it, phases, and also rules to the "game". Our biggest failure to having a healthy relationship is confusing being "in love" with LOVE; they are so far from being the same thing. Being in love requires only a shallow and circumstantial mix of emotions. Being in love is that spark of attraction, that daydream of romance, or that tingle up your spine (and let's be honest sisters, often in our panties). Don't get me wrong, those feelings are important and help us to recognize a potential partner. However, the feeling of being in love neither builds a true foundation, nor does it sustain a relationship through the trials and adversity that it will no doubt be forced to endure.

Love, on the other hand, requires depth, time, devotion, and commitment. I've come to understand that love is not a feeling nor an idea, it is an intentional ACT of pre-determined decisions and sacrifices chosen for the ultimate purpose of protecting and providing for the benefit of another (whew, that's a mouthful). Many people are ignorant to the fact that God, our creator who is indeed LOVE and modeled love incarnate through Jesus Christ, also defined what love is in His Word (1 Corinthians 13:4-8).

Understanding that love is something that one does and because of their action, another can feel that expression of love, is paramount to being in a healthy, loving relationship; but it starts with showing love to yourself. This is where I struggled in my desire to find love: I for one, didn't really know God, and I failed to know how to love myself first. Most of the dating relationships and even marriages that we see in our family or friend groups, or displayed on television and social media would fail to pass the test if required to meet the standards of love according to the One who created it. The proof that we don't really understand that LOVE is an action and not a feeling is evident in the high rates of divorce and intimate partner abuse; and what's worse is many go from failed relationship to failed relationship without knowing any better. According to the American Psychological Association, *"approximately 40-50% of first marriages end in divorce with approximately 60-67% of second marriages ending in divorce."* What we don't know the first time, many obviously don't take the time to learn for the second…sad but true!

So, sister, here's the deal, in relationships, what you don't KNOW can and will hurt you. If you (and your partner) don't truly know what love is and you don't show it to yourself first, you will always feel inadequate, unworthy, and unwanted. You should not have to fight to have the person you are "in love" with show you love and vice versa. Someone putting their hands on you, cursing you out, demeaning and humiliating you, being jealous of you, controlling your actions: what you wear, how you talk, and even how you spend your time and your money, is NOT love, it's control. The need to control others comes from fear and Sis, love does NOT fear!

So how can you determine if you are being loved or simply in-love? Just like we know if a handbag or a pair of Red Bottoms is authentic or a knockoff; we check it against the original design.

According to 1 Corinthians 13:4-8 LOVE IS:

Patient: *is the relationship (intimacy) moving at a pace that feels comfortable for you, or are you feeling rushed? Is he "love bombing" you, wanting to get intimate right out the gate?*

Kind: *does he do and say nice things for/to you: cook, clean, give gifts, say affirming things, consider your needs and interests, or whatever you find kind (without expecting sex or anything in return)?*

It does not envy: *Does he support your dreams, talents, and encourage you to be your best or does he make you feel insecure or question your loyalty to him when you want to do things without him or with other people? Is he dismissive of your accomplishments or others compliments of you?*

It does not boast: *Is he constantly talking about what he does for you or others; demanding you show appreciation or be submissive because of what he does, or who he is?*

It is not proud: *Does he accept responsibility (apologizes) when he does wrong or hurts your feelings? Is he willing to ask for help, or seek criticism and advice from others, even you?*

It does not dishonor others: *Does he put you down or call you out of your name? Does he disrespect you: lie, cheat, or still?*

It is not self-seeking: *Does he seek your best interest in his decisions, and does he communicate that with you, or does he do what he wants and expect you to just go along?*

It is not easily angered: *Does he quickly get angry and irritated by what you do or say, and does he blame you for making him mad?*

It keeps no record of wrongs: *Does he bring up things you said or did to make you feel guilty or ashamed or to get you to do what he wants?*

Love does not delight in evil but rejoices with the truth: *Does he find other's failures or embarrassment to be funny? Does he say "I told you so" or "that's what you get" when something doesn't go your way or when you are hurt or offended by others?*

It always protects: *If you desire to be married, but you've been dating for a few years (or already have kids together) and he has no set plan to marry you, what's the hold up? Sis, being officially married provides protection for one another in the case of death (legally, financially, and emotionally). Does he defend you and your character (even from his mama)? Does he tell your secrets; does he make you feel safe?*

Always trusts: *Does he question your decisions? Does he get jealous of who you hang out with?*

Always hopes: *Does he seek the best for your future together? Does he plan for it?*

Always perseveres: *Does he shut down, lash out, or walk out when disagreements/conflict arise? Is he there through your adversities and even failures, comforting you when you're sick, by your side through job/family losses?*

Love never fails: *Do you have clear and agreed upon expectations of one another, and you find that you both intentionally work to deliver, or are you consistently disappointed? Does he show up when he says he will, do what he says he will do, take accountability for what he is responsible for?*

Sis, take time to ask whether you do these things for him as well, and more importantly, for YOURSELF. Remember, what you don't know about love CAN and WILL hurt. Loving others requires you to know and love yourself first!

Lady Dawn Runyon is a native of Huntsville, AL, and a Veteran of the United States Army. Dawn holds a Bachelor's degree from the University of Kentucky, in Integrated Strategic Communications.

She currently resides in Lexington, KY with her husband, and their two young adult sons. As an only child born to a young teen mom and absent father, Dawn has overcome many of life's struggles, including childhood sexual abuse and domestic violence. She works as a domestic & sexual violence prevention specialist implementing a bystander intervention program.

Dawn is also a Neighborhood Healers Fellow, encouraging and supporting Mental Health awareness in the Black Community.

Her two devotional books, *Living LYTE (memoir devotional)* and *W.O.W. Words of Wisdom*, are set for future release. As an author, inspirational speaker, life coach, and ordained minister, she has retained one goal throughout her Marketplace Ministry, Dawn's LYTE: to empower others to experience the abundant life found in a relationship with Christ.

She can be found on Facebook and Instagram at "Dawnslyte" and contacted via email at dawnslyte@gmail.com.

MINISTERING ON BROKEN PIECES

Elder Sherri M. Lea

April 14th, 2020 @ 5:27 a.m. The morning that changed my life forever.

I heard "Sherri get up, something is wrong." I thought I was dreaming because Bruce was supposed to be gone to work already. I heard it again, "Sherri get up something is wrong." Immediately I jumped to my feet; my husband is in trouble was all I could think, and immediately I begin to pray, because if prayer is not your first response it needs to be your second response. "Lord my husband is in trouble, Lord I bind COVID-19, and I release in healing in the Mighty Name of Jesus." Little did I know this morning would change my relationship status for life, change my mind, my heart, and my home.

All I knew is that my husband was in trouble. "Babe what's wrong?" I asked. In a very faint voice, he said, "I don't know.

I've never felt like this." He said, "I feel like I need to throw up." Hurriedly, I found something for him to regurgitate in. As he experienced reflux, I saw his eyes roll back into his head and he blacked out. When he regained consciousness, I saw fear in his eyes. "EMS is on the way, hold on, babe." My thoughts shifted to, "I can't help because I don't know what to do." Prayer is the only thing I knew to do. When EMS arrived, the rescue personnel checked his vital signs, which were stable, but they could not get an oxygen count. The rescuers stated, "Mr. Lea, we know what it's not, but we have to get you to the hospital in order to determine what it is."

I heard my husband say, "*I need to throw up.*" He started gagging again, and he fell forward. The very last words I heard him whisper were, "*Jesus Help Me.*"

Immediately, the paramedics knew they had to get Bruce to the hospital as soon as possible. I could hear them ask, "Mr. Lea, can you hear me?" The rescuers provided step by step details on what procedures they were taking to help him; but they were unable to lift him onto the gurney because his body was solid. One of the EMS workers called on reinforcements to help lift Bruce off the floor to the chair by our stairs. In the distance, I heard more sirens. It was the fire department. My mind racing, in a fog, I listened to their conversations. "This guy is a beast, not fat, but solid muscle." Continuing to instruct him about what is going on, they were able to get him to the front porch then I heard them say, "Mr. Lea, we need your help, you have to help us stand you up, so we can get you onto the stretcher." However, my other half continuing gagging and blacking out. Quickly, the paramedics rushed my husband down our driveway because he was dying. This was the beginning of my Bruce's transition into eternal life.

The next thirteen days consisted of nothing but reflection and conversations with God. I asked, "God, did I do something wrong as a wife to cause this? God, did he do something wrong as a husband to cause this? But God, you said that Bruce would be my husband, and that we would do ministry together!" God's reply was, "Sherri I did what I said, Bruce is your husband, you served in ministry together before you got married and after, all the other plans were yours." I pleaded, "But God, he doesn't deserve this." "Sherri he's ready."

April 24, 2020

The neurologist called to say, "Mrs. Lea, I am going to be completely honest with you; Bruce will never be the same, he will never come back home. Now is the time to make some decisions, speak with your family and we will meet on Monday."

April 27th @ 10:00 a.m.

In disbelief, I hung up the phone and dropped to my knees, weeping and pleading, "GOD, HE DOESN'T DESERVE THIS!" "SHERRI, WHO ARE YOU TO TELL ME WHAT HE DESERVES?" "He is ready," was all I heard. Instantly, a calm enveloped the room. I begin to thank and praise God for the time we had together; for everything we did in ministry and our marriage - the good, bad, and ugly… it was all worth it. Immediately, I forgot about myself and began praying for our family, children, siblings, grandchildren, and others. There is a special strength that comes from a praying wife/mother, this is the day I had to accept what God allowed, take Him by the hand and trust Him to carry me through what could have destroyed me.

I remember saying to myself, "*I cannot believe I waited until I was 51 years old to get married and now I am about to be a widow, where's the Glory in that?*"

"*Trust the process to Purpose*"

That morning I signed papers allowing the medical staff to remove my other half, the head of the house, my lover, and friend from life support. I was not ready emotionally, but I knew it was time to say, "See you later, my dear." My friends would not let me go alone; they accompanied me to Cone Hospital and sat in the parking lot until I finished. The support I received from them was amazing. My support system has been strong, and I thank God for my friends and Pastor being there for me when I needed them most. As I listened to my husband transition, I thanked him for being the good husband, father, and friend to so many, and I watched him slip away into eternal life. At that moment, God wrapped me in His unfailing love and said, "It's time to do ministry." It is a different type of strength needed to minister from Broken Pieces; especially, when you must keep going, and you want to stop; when you cannot speak, and you are just numb, but you hear the Lord downloading a message inside your spirit as you are planning your husband's homecoming service.

WHAT DO YOU DO WHEN YOU HAVE TO MINISTER ON BROKEN PIECES? Beloved, you trust His hand when you do not understand His plan.

Elder Sherri M. Lea is a native of Greensboro NC. She is the widow to the late Bruce Wayne Lea of Burlington NC. mother of two and four grandchildren. She graduated from North Carolina School of Theology with an Associates and bachelor's degree in Theology. She is an ordained Minister and Outreach Coordinator at the Tabernacle of Meeting, under the leadership of Pastor Russell Miller, in Greensboro. Sherri is the CEO of She'Lea Designs' where fashion design is her passion, and she is a skilled tailor. Sherri is a military veteran, from the US Army. She is a woman of faith and integrity, who practices what she preaches, and gives all the honor and glory to God. This is her first published work.

She can be contacted via Facebook.

JUST BREATHE: ENHANCING YOUR LIFE BY RESTING IN GOD

Minister Teresa Ekundayo

One of the most important things we need to learn is how to rest in God. Without the ability to rest in God, everything else is out of order. The inability to rest spiritually usually results in an inabilty to rest physically and mentally. This failure to rest causes inconsistency in our thoughts, actions, and responses, disrupting our flow with God. Think back to a stressful time you experienced something that made you feel like you should have said or reacted differently, however, in that moment you were momentarily stunned. Sometimes situations *"knock the wind"* out of us and we lack the words and 'breath' to respond appropriately. These are the circumstances we need to be able to hand over to God and learn how to rest completely in Him and *just breathe*!

Sis! We breathe! Animals breathe. Plants breathe. Maybe we should scratch that last one. The point is, we all breathe!

Thankfully, God gifted us with a very important feature called breathing. In the beginning of creation, God fashioned us with His own hands, but, there was one missing element we still needed for life … Breath. According to Genesis 2:7[i], it was after God formed man that he *"breathed into his nostrils the breath of life."* It wasn't until this act that man became a living soul. What a miracle! Can we just take a praise break right here? Look at Genesis 7:22[ii]. After Noah and his family endured the great flood, the scripture states *"All in whose nostrils was the breath of life, of all that was in the dry land, died".* Now look at Job 27:3[iii] *"All the while my breath is in me, and the spirit of God is in my nostrils".* All three of these scriptures show us that life connects to breathing and breath comes from God.

Initially, each of us were created to breathe in an unimpeded manner. What am I saying here? Originally, ladies, we were able to breathe freely without any type of hinderances. The functions of our lungs, nostrils, emotions, and will were in an untainted state until the fall of man. One of the Hebrew definitions of breathe is *Yaphach* meaning (3306)[iv] to breathe or "puff". We refer to the word Yaphach when we breathe in a forced manner. This is the style of breath we use when someone has gotten on our "last nerve" or we are angry and frustrated. Jeremiah 4:31*v* refers to the *Yaphach* style of breathing when it compares the cries of an unfaithful Judah to a woman in labor for the first time gasping for breath. *Naphash* (5314)[vi], another Hebrew definition for breathe, means "to be refreshed, to breathe passively, to be breathed upon, refreshed (as if by a current of air)." God commanded us to be refreshed on the Sabbath day in Exodus 23:12[vii]. This breathing style comes with ease and is similar to a cold glass of water on a 98° day. *Yaphach* (forced breath) is a necessary part of our existence, but, God prefers for us to live in the *Naphash* (passive, refreshed) version of breath.

Certain physical states of unrest cause our breathing to be interrupted. One of these states of unrest is stress. Although most of us consider breathing as just a lung function, there is a mental connection, a level of capability required to breathe, and there is life in the ability to breathe. Stress is a situation in which we experience an abnormal amount of pressure emotionally, physically, or sometimes both. Think about how you react in a stressful situation. Can you recall if your breathing changed? Was your breathing quicker and shorter? Most likely it was. This is a normal occurrence when we are dealing with a difficult situation or we have just exited a deeply traumatic moment. Stressors are not necessarily bad, they provide warning signs that certain situations are conditions we should exit; however, constant stress was not the plan God designed.

Next, ladies let us discuss two states of unrest that for our purposes I would like to call "the twin cousins" of stress. These two twins are fear and anxiety. Shock temporarily disrupts us, but, fear and anxiety can paralyze us. Imagine what happens physically when an unexpected person startles you or you are suddenly thrust into a disturbing position. For example, I received a video from a friend in which a gruesome figure unexpectantly leaped out in 3D while screeching horribly! Immediately I inhaled sharply and I stopped breathing momentarily. My simultaneous response was to jump, kick my legs as if I were swimming, scream, and throw my cell phone. Thank God I splurged on a good phone case. Our fight-or-flight response is normal in most cases. My reaction was definitely hilarious afterwards, but, it was a completely normal response given the situation. That example was a temporary instance, but, many women live like this daily, which is not normal. That fear often keeps them from taking the next step, walking into their purpose, asking for the raise, letting go of dead situations, and totally trusting God.

Some women live with anxiety that comes from the need for validation or from excessive worry. They are so concerned about what would be said if they attempt something new or what would happen if they honor their own feelings instead of the people they are so strenuously trying to please. Sometimes unresolved grief can morph itself into anxiety. Grief must be processed and takes time because we are human, but, often times we throw ourselves into our job, comfort food, or other "busy-ness" quiet the pain that only God can heal. Anxiety causes our muscles to tense and our breathing becomes labored (Yaphach). Anxiety can be on a consistent level, but, it can also be an attack. This is an instance where you are literally gripped with fear and all your body functions cease to function normally. Your breathing is forced and rapid causing an imbalance in your oxygen levels. We have entered a state of flowing with what the enemy would desire for us rather than the peace that God provides – characterized by a rapid heart rate, elevated blood pressure, headache, cold sweats, and a state of heightened panic.

Stress, fear, and anxiety effect our health and we spend more time going to the doctor, popping pills, or praying for a healing that has a root that has not been addressed. This is definitely not what God designed for us. There are spiritual implications to the physical states of unrest we experience consistently. Things that occur in the natural will manifest into things in the Spirit. In Genesis, the wind of God on our physical man gave life and became life to our Spirit. In order to eliminate stress, anxiety, and abnormal fear, we should give God his job back! It was never our job to bear these burdens. Remember, we discussed earlier that the *functions of our lungs, nostrils, emotions, and will were in an untainted state until the fall of man*? We have to return to the initial state God gave us in the garden where our rest is in Him and our breath (the Spirit of God in our nostrils) is unhindered.

How do we return back to that initial state of rest from the garden ladies? Jesus gave us specific instructions and warnings that will help us in 1 Peter 5:6-9[viii] "*Humble yourselves, therefore, under God's mighty hand, that he may lift you up in due time. Cast all your anxiety on him because he cares for you. Be alert and of sober mind. Your enemy the devil prowls around like a roaring lion looking for someone to devour. Resist him, standing firm in the faith, because you know that the family of believers throughout the world is undergoing the same sufferings.*" Our instructions are to humble ourselves, cast our anxiety on him, be alert, sober-minded, and to resist the devil. Look for areas of pride in your life. Do a self inventory for any areas where you may have taken a matter into your own hands and out of the hands of the God. Cast your anxieties on Him. Look for any areas where you have possibly placed your need for validation in the wrong place. Are you looking for validation in man, in a certain position, a title, or in your job? Cast out fear! Fear is a distraction. Think about the areas that are being hindered by fear. What is it that the enemy is trying to keep you from progressing in due to fear? Are you walking in the full calling of God? Is fear causing you to be stagnant? Take a moment to consider your current situations. In what areas have you left room for doubt? In what circumstances is the enemy whispering to you and making you think you are the only one going through a certain trial?

We know that our Father has everything under control. What are you worried about? Think back to times when you thought it was definitely "the end" because you didn't have the money, or couldn't get the job, or whatever the situation may have been. Did it not work out somehow? Aren't you still here? Just breathe Sis! If it worked out before, it will work out again. It may not have worked exactly as WE planned, but, it is God's plans we should be concerned about because He knows the plans he has for us! God is not trying to harm us. He has plans to prosper us. (see Jeremiah 29:11)[ix]. Striving is not our portion! We have the authority of ease! Decree and declare: *We will live in the Napash, refreshing, breathed upon instance of God's breath. We dwell in the peace that surpasses all understanding! We will not be swayed by circumstances and the things of this world. We will enhance our lives by resting in God.* I encourage you to ask God to help you return to the state of His original gift of rest for your life. It is in this state of rest that you can finally breathe and everything you need to accomplish can be accomplished while resting."

CREDIT CHECK: TIPS FOR TURNING YOUR CREDIT ZERO INTO A CREDIT HERO

Minister Teresa Ekundayo

When I was a little girl, I wasn't very knowledgeable about credit; **I thought that people bought things to enjoy now, and someone magically paid the bill later**. In our community there was a convenience store where everyone in the neighborhood would go to get basic items, such as gas, cooked to order food, and snacks. My mom would shop there often. She would say tell a gentleman, whom I will call Gary, to put things on her tab, and he would reply "no problem". Gary would whip out his little leather-bound with manila colored pages' ledger book and flip to my dad's name. He would ring up the items and make an entry into his little book. I accompanied my parents when one of them would pay on what they owed. It was then that I understood that meant there was still a balance due. Being older now, I realize that was one of my first experiences with credit.

As life continued, I learned some things from various training, certifications, research, and life experiences about credit that I will summarize in the paragraphs below. Knowing what credit is and how it works will allow us to count the costs of credit and make better financial decisions, turning our credit zeroes to credit heroes!

What is credit? You may already know this answer, but for our ladies who are not as well-versed, let's define it so we can all be on the same level of understanding as we discuss credit. Credit has more than one meaning. We will focus on three meanings for credit, all of which will apply to our discussion today. According to Investopedia, *"Credit is generally defined as an agreement between a lender and a borrower, Credit also refers to an individual or business' creditworthiness or credit history. In accounting, a credit may either decrease assets or increase liabilities as well as decrease expenses or increase revenue."*[i] Going back to my experiences at Gary's convenience store, I witnessed the first description of credit. My parents were good people and well known in the community. Based solely on their character, they could purchase things and pay at a later date. Most adults over thirty-five would be familiar with this type of credit exchange as a child. You would be familiar with "tabs", furniture stores, and the sales magazines which offered the 'enjoy now, pay later' structure. The second meaning of credit is the one most of us are aware of. To receive credit currently, your character doesn't really hold any weight; instead, your discipline in making sure you pay your bills on time, your ability to borrow an amount and pay it off, and your credit history are what creditors look for. The third definition is when an amount is credited or subtracted from the balance owed. We like this definition the most. The more credits we receive, the less we owe.

We can separate credits into good and bad categories. To the average consumer, when you whip out your card to pay for that Starbucks latte, it doesn't seem to make any difference. In fact, the purchases you make on your credit cards matter. When planning for a major purchase like a house, some creditors will not only look at how you spend and how you pay, but also what you purchase. If you have a habit of charging fast food meals, lattes, and groceries on your credit cards, some creditors will see that as an inability to pay for your common needs. Items like a student loan, a home purchase, a new kitchen appliance, an automobile purchase are some examples of what would be considered good purchases. These purchases are not everyday purchases, and creditors would expect to see these types of items.

Carrying a balance and only paying the minimum amount, having too many accounts open, and not having accounts old enough to be deemed as "established" affect your credit. Your credit "worthiness" is a delicate balance and requires strategic practices to reach and maintain a good credit score. When I worked for a corporate mortgage company many years ago, one job I had was pulling 20 years of credit and analyzing the creditworthiness of the individual who had applied for a home. There were certain items that the company required that they be notified of. It was a very time-consuming process where the individual had to prove why certain items in the report should be overlooked and, in some cases, provide reasoning why those items were even there. Every company is different, but there are some basic rules you need to stay familiar with.

According to Experian, "The base FICO Scores range from 300 to 850, and FICO defines the 'good range as 670 to 739.'" "FICO considers scoring factors in the following order:

> Payment History 35%
> Amounts Owed 30%
> Length of credit History 15%
> Credit mix: 10%
> New Credit 10%"[ii]

As I mentioned before, each company may have their set of requirements to gain a credit approval. In my experience, although there may be a certain order and percentage listed that make up your credit score, there are some things that really affect your score the greatest and the fastest. The quickest way to take your credit score from good to bad and from bad to good is by maintaining your credit balances. For instance, let us pretend you have 4 credit cards with a $500 balance and 3 of those cards hold a balance due of $350 and one of those is maxed out at $500. Out of a total credit line of $2,000, you have used $1,550 of the $2,000. If you check your credit score, you will notice you will lose a good deal of points while holding these balances. In reverse, if you only use $100 of the $2,000, and you pay that off every month, it may guarantee that your score will go higher. You accomplish two tricks of credit in the latter example. You show that your credit revolves, meaning you may make a purchase, but you can pay that off. Secondly, your credit ratio, the amount available verse the amount spent, looks better to creditors and shows that you have the credit, but you are not a "wasteful" consumer.

Another area you want to get under control, if you have not already, is your payment history. Many people are guilty of knowing a bill is due and "riding" the grace period, even if that means you pay a small fee to "buy yourself" a few more days. If this is you, just say ouch and make that a habit you stop. Your payment history will take a sizeable chunk out of your score if it is not managed properly. You also want to examine what kinds of credit accounts you have. It may not seem to be a big deal, but you should aim to have different types of credit accounts. This is what they refer to as a credit mix. Ideally, you should have a mix of long-term credit such as loans mixed in with things like credit cards. This strongly suggests that you are a credible consumer, and you can maintain yourself in different areas, and this accountability can reflect in your credit score.

The length of time your credit accounts have been open and maintained will matter a lot. You will notice this if you were to pay off a credit card or a loan. The average expectation is that your credit score would go up because paying off credit is a good thing. Right? In most cases, your credit will immediately take a dip. It may adjust itself in one to two credit bureau reporting cycles, but, most likely, it will be lower than it was before you paid the account off. This is because it may have affected your length of time with active credit. For example, if Charlene paid off her student loan, and it was maintained and started 10 years ago, her length of credit history adjusts to the next item still relevant on her report. If Charlene's next item is, let us say an auto loan maintained for 4 years, her credit history adjusts to that time frame. Her longest active account is now 4 years old, versus the 10-year student loan. This would explain the change in your credit score.

Lastly, just say NO to the cashier that is offering a 20% discount if you open an account with them today. I know you can get another discount off the outfit you are purchasing at the door buster sale, but, slowly back away from spontaneous credit offers. Each time you apply for one of these offers, even if you don't get approved, you have a "hard" inquiry on your report. Too many of these make you look like you are desperate for credit. This is similar to a man we have all seen at some point trying to hit on every lady at the company party before he finally arrives in front of you with too much cologne. Random applications make you look like the man at the company party, and you can understand why they would say no when you come to them for credit. Although it looks better to have a certain amount of history with different accounts, you want to make sure you only apply for new credit when you don't have a choice. New credit accounts also cause a credit score to dip. Occasionally, it will correct itself, but it will all depend on your overall credit situation.

Do not get excited about the fact that a company offered you an opportunity for credit, get excited when you are fully aware of all the details and know exactly how much that credit will cost. When you pay on a credit card, only part of that payment goes to the actual balance (principle) of your card. The other portion goes to interest. Bad credit makes you pay more for everything that requires credit. A credit card purchase of a refrigerator at $1,000 with 0% interest for 12 months on a planned expense only costs you the amount of the purchased item if you pay it off in the 12 months. Let's look at that same purchase using Credit Karma's credit card repayment calculator using a credit card with an interest rate of 29%. Your principal would be $1,041 along with an interest rate of $59 for a total of $1,100.[iii] You may look at this simple example and say, $100 that's not bad, but these instances add up. That $100 could have been spent or invested elsewhere.

Bad credit is an invitation to embarrassing phone calls at work and harassing phone calls at home. Credit collection companies make a lot of money securing payment when the company itself did not have the time and resources to recoup the loss. Some of these agencies buy your account from the company and are very ruthless in obtaining payment. Be careful answering questions on negative items that have according to credit rules aged off your credit report. Collection agencies can take simple items like you saying yes to your name being correct or verifying your personal information as your willingness to discuss the debt, and they can restart the clock on old items. This means they can add items that have aged off your report back. You want to make sure this is something you don't have to experience. If it is something you are going through now, after you resolve the issues, the phone will stop ringing and the letters will soon stop.

Here are a few things to keep in mind to help you gain ground in credit. You want to adjust your mindset if you haven't already to pay before or on the due date. For example, including an extra $15 on a bill due every two weeks for a year would amount to and extra $365 of payments that year on the principle." $1 extra on a $50 payment over a year is an extra $365 of payments that year on the principle. This also puts you in good standing for a no penalty payment deferment should the need ever arise. Save up for purchases and search for deals instead of borrowing when possible. If you plan to make the purchase on a credit card, have a plan on how and when you will pay it off. Take advantage of no interest offers, but be careful to pay the whole balance before for the time stated ends, or the amount of interest you would have paid will be added to your balance. Use online calculators to find out how much you will actually pay for what you purchase. If you are planning to buy a house or making a large purchase, ask to see someone at your local bank. Explain to them, you want to have a "soft inquiry" meaning it does not affect your credit score as a hit. Most financial institutions can pull a soft inquiry of your report and show you the areas that you will need to work on. Their advice is invaluable as this will probably be the same institution you come to when you need said loan.

Do some research, hire someone, or join a group to find out which credit items would benefit your credit if you paid it off. Research how to negotiate with the creditors, dispute incorrect items with your credit bureau, and write credit letters for removal of negative items after payment. Afterward, call up your creditors and negotiate to pay negative items off. Sometimes creditors will offer a payoff amount at a significant discount from the balance owed. Even if you are receiving calls or notices or phone calls from a collection agency, bypass them and go straight to the company you owe for negotiation. Only negotiate with the collection agency if you have no other choice. Many of the original creditors have long since written off these balances and don't expect to get anything back from them. You are taking the initiative, explaining your situation, and your willingness to pay off these old debts usually works out well.

Recovering from a poor credit score is not the easiest task, but, with consistent work, it can be done. Your credit zero score can become a credit hero score, but it will take some effort. Do not get discouraged and celebrate every new point. Soon your score will be miles from where you started. Years ago, because of a terrible phase of sickness, I lost everything, including my place of residence. My truck was repossessed, I couldn't afford to pay the rent, I was evicted, and my utilities were disconnected. You name it and it happened! I thought it was the worst thing in the world. God knew it was not the worst thing in the world, although it was very embarrassing for me. I was a credit zero! God already knew he equipped with the knowledge basics of credit. I can now take what I put into practice through his guidance to get myself back on my feet and share that with others. Not only did God help me get myself back in right standing, but I went from renting and on the verge of homelessness to being a homeowner built from the ground up. Wow! What a God we serve! I am now a credit hero, and hopefully, you are too. If not, please follow the simple steps above and you should be on your way! Take what you learn and share it with others. I am rooting for you, Sis! I celebrate you in advance!

Minister Teresa Carroll Ekundayo journey began in ministry serving in the church from a young age. She is an ordained Minister and Associate Pastor, dedicated to serving others with her natural gift for teaching and helping. With over 20 years of experience in the corporate industry, Teresa has worked alongside executive leaders, managing complex projects, multi-million-dollar accounts, and spearheading credit research. Her expertise includes creating innovative solutions and providing training in personal development.

As the founder of TMWT Coaching & Consulting, Teresa funnels her passion for empowering Christian women to live in abundance and impact. Through her online coaching company, she guides women towards personal and spiritual growth, equipping them to make a positive difference in their communities and beyond.

Teresa is also an accomplished author; with her book "*My Financial Journal*" available on Amazon, she offers practical insights into financial management and stewardship. For more inspiration, accountability, and guidance, visit Teresa's website at www.2minswithteresa.org, where she continues to inspire and uplift others so they can live in abundance and walk in purpose that impacts others.

[i] Brock, Thomas (March 2021) Credit. Retrieved from https://www.investopedia.com/terms/c/credit.asp

[ii] What is good credit. Retrieved from" https://www.experian.com/blogs/ask-experian/credit-education/score-basics/what-is-a-good-credit-score/

[iii] Debt Repayment Calculator. Retrieved from: https://www.creditkarma.com/calculators/debtrepayment

FINDING ME

Prophetess Charlene Stinson

Anthony Hamilton stated, "And the point of it All…" Although he stated this from the aspect of relationships, my current viewpoint is the following: what is the point of things we endure and situations we must embrace? What is the purpose of the pain and agony many faces daily or the rhetoric of life in general? Why can't situations be easier and why did our flesh have to be so selfish, self—centered, hard-headed and disobedient? These are questions that have remained in my mind throughout periods of my life, and even more so, in this present season of my Life.

This part is hard for me, and at times it feels impossible to press amidst the chaos. However, I recognize that I must press forward for the impossible to become possible.

Often, I have pondered the following questions: *Who am I? Why was I born? Why am I here? Am I seen? Am I causing change to occur? Have I and am I a threat to the Kingdom of Darkness? Do I still appear timid? Who do people see when focusing on me? My husband, the Lord? How much time do I really have? Why have I wasted so much time? Why does it seem that so many things have been placed on hold for me? What was the point in trying to do things in order, all for my life at 39 to be difficult and not being able to see the direction it could have been in?* These questions plague my mind often, practically every day. There are times where I feel so paralyzed (present moment) that life does not seem enjoyable. Honestly, it is hard to climb out of that place when you have been there for so long! It is even harder when the expectations of what you thought was going to be seems nearly impossible to accomplish.

Being the eldest child, I always believed in having morals, values, and that Integrity should always be part of your name. It is who you are. It is what you stand for. Whether words are spoken or not, having Integrity displays your inner being. Although they are great to have, this trait means nothing if your heart is not aligned with our Creator. And without believing in who HE is, we are merely existing with no hope in sight, no direction, and in honesty, no reason to live.

Quiet and caring were two strengths that describe my personality. There were however, three traits I hid and was too embarrassed to be reveal: *Jealousy, low self-esteem, and inadequacy*. And these three developed into *lust of the eyes*. At one point, I came to accept that if I never grew into being accepted by anyone, that this spirit would be enough. *I know extremely Dangerous Concept*! The scripture Hosea 4:6-7 is true when it states the following, "*My people perish for lack of knowledge…*" Lacking knowledge and having low confidence

I could not imagine either of these aforementioned character traits being more significant than the other. Each of them was just as significant for me.

As a child, I was always the heaviest, and when entering middle and high school, I was always the friend of someone who boys wanted, not *The One that others were attracted to*. As I grew in the Lord and learned his Word, I felt more secure in knowing who I was and who I am, but my negative thoughts about myself still haunted me when being amongst others who seemed to be more confident; who seemed to possess the essence of Favor, simplicity, and who it seemed that everyone *flocked* to, because of their outward appearance.

The definition of jealousy, according to Merriam Webster is, **"the thoughts or feelings of insecurity, fear and concern over a relative lack of possessions or safety, and can also result in anger, resentment, inadequacy, helplessness or disgust."** Jealousy ... *Whew*. Jealousy is not an emotion to be proud of, yet it is a feeling that "pops up" at the most inopportune times. Additionally, I refer to jealousy as "the art of jealousy," providing it with a personal. In my opinion, The *Art of Jealousy* comes in different forms. Jealousy brings corruption and defeat if given the opportunity. Personally, I believe jealousy causes separation and division, not allowing the true essence of a person to be seen, and causes the possibility of deliverance to be rejected. So, what is the next step in the ***Art of Jealousy***? In my personal and ministerial experience, it is to maintain the desire and strength to continue being fed lies of deceit; trying to overpower and possess the mind in not acknowledging that The one that lives in the individual (me or you) is Greater than the one that lives in the world (the enemy). Despite knowing this, jealousy continued to embark on a journey of attempting to overtake me, my future, my relationships, and my life.

To add more fuel to the fire, along with jealousy there was low self- esteem in my life. Spiritually, I believe this was in my bloodline. Low self-esteem is described as a lack of confidence in oneself and his or her abilities; this may include feelings of incompetence, being unloved or inadequate. According to *Psychology Today*, "*Life experiences and emotions create that sense within us in a variety of ways. As Adults, armed with education on emotions and how childhood adversity affects the brain, we can understand that feeling "not enough is a byproduct of an environment that was insufficient. It continues stating that those who struggle with low self-esteem are consistently afraid about making mistakes or letting others down.*" I must say that I knew I was loved, yet, at times I did not feel like I was enough.

In later years, emotional manipulation and control introduced itself, thus delaying me realizing my identity. Manipulation presented as beautiful and fruitful but *was later exposed* as entrapment. According to Merriam-Webster, *manipulation is to control (command, restrain, or manage) or play upon by artful, unfair, or insidious means especially to one's own advantage.* I once heard someone say, "*I manipulate others so that they can see the good in themselves.*" The manipulator fails to understand how he or she is being manipulated as well.

What happens when these two spirits (manipulation and control) are exposed? They fight even harder to make sure that the individual being controlled does not make the decision in being freed and that the individual's feelings are placed aside for the controller to remain comfortable in their behavior. Manipulation and control come as a pair; signs include fear, obligation, guilt, questioning yourself, strings being attached, judging or criticizing actions, causing or making one to feel indebted and many other signs. These are generally accepted and socially recognized across disciplines.

For me, these behaviors led to settling in angry places where my mind created thoughts, and from those thoughts imaginary *kingdoms or strongholds* were formed. I gave those spiritual obstacles life by constantly focusing on them as opposed to casting them down in my mind. My mindset had formed this "fake reality," and from that point, decisions were being made from false reality. One thought from what my mind relayed to my eyes led to multiple thoughts and these thoughts then had conversations with themselves. These conversations led to me engaging with different personalities. Yes, this sounds crazy and unreal, but it was as real as going into the grocery store and trying to decide which meat you were going to get based off the stores' deal for the month. They intertwined like a rope, with no separation, and the desire of one's purpose to not be fulfilled. These moments caused mental turmoil, confusion and blindness to the Written Word spoken in my life. This was true spiritual warfare for me.

Many people have endured countless situations that have propelled them into their destinies. And many have had moments of no longer wanting to walk into their purpose due to their pain being traumatic that can only be explained using derogatory language.

Despite all this, each day brings sunshine; whether it is seen or not and the trees are standing tall. The trees are areas that we must all face, including life's uncertainties, maneuvering through situations that seem impossible and creating strategies that help us see life for what it could really be, exciting and beautiful.

Overall, a moment of desperation must take place for change to occur. My moment of desperation occurred after having my children and these moments continue evolving daily. It is only in Christ Jesus that I live, move and have my being. I know, in Him, I am enough.

This mere thought and acceptance did not occur overnight. I had to fully understand and embrace this for myself. I needed to acknowledge that my identity is hidden in Christ! I had to come into agreement with this and know that God placed His attributes within me, and because I am created in His image and likeness, I am enough.

Now Faith …

According to Hebrews 11:1, *"Now faith is the assurance of things hoped for and the conviction of things not seen."* What are you believing God for while amid darkness and despair? What has God spoken that may have been hidden by the season that you are currently in? You must realize that your purpose lies in the Most High's Heart. His Plan for us was shaped with delicacy, care and concern, or precise thought.

We must believe that this thing called life is a puzzle in which the Creator has placed the pieces together perfectly. His never-ending love is the glue making sure that the pieces remain intertwined. Knowing who you are can only be found in knowing who The Most-High is and that is enough. I may have had some things almost overtake me; but those things helped define the woman I am and mature to a new level. I have not arrived and I still have some growing to do; I will not stop growing into the person God has created me to be.

Now faith... I must have faith to believe that the work He started, He will complete in me. Until then, I'll continue believing His established Word, assist with advancing the Kingdom, and allow the Lord's Purpose to be fulfilled.

Dearest beloved, believe Him and know that every thought, moment, circumstance, event, assignment, feeling, and tear will shape your purpose and establish your identity in Christ.

Prophetess Charlene Stinson-Hill resides in Lancaster, South Carolina. While growing up, she began playing piano through the instruction of Carolyn Petroski, and it was at this moment that her teacher recognized something greater than talent present. She continued grooming this gift, and Charlene continued playing throughout high school. She originally majored in Music in college; however, later changed to Social Work. Then music was no longer a part of the gifting she pursued, due to hurtful events she experienced which hampered her growth in this ministry. Charlene graduated from South Carolina State University with a Bachelor of Arts Degree in Social Work in 2003 and continued pursuing educational opportunities by receiving a Master of Arts Degree in Rehabilitation Counseling in 2006. As times and ministries changed, she faced painful events that contributed to her longer wanting to play the piano. But Glory be to God, deliverance took place, and the Gifting of Prophetic Worship and Scribal Prophet were birthed. In 2010, Charlene married

Apostle Russell Hill. The couple has four children - Christian, Addison, Zoey, and Kinsley.

Charlene enjoys spending time with family, playing the piano, and writing in her spare time. In 2018, she received her Honorary Doctorate in Music under Yeshiva Worship Ministry. She works at New Hope Treatment Facility, which provides specialized treatment to traumatized children and young adults.

Charlene's desire is to see people not only exist but to live, and to see the desires of our Father's Heart be fulfilled through His people.

REMEMBER ME

Minister Matokia Brown

We as women have struggled privately for so long. We have privately struggled through so many things without the presence of reliable help that we've learned to accomplish our trials quickly and alone. Furthermore, we've become masters at problem-solving; a professional "solutionist" if you will. Through multiple disappointments we've morphed into iron clad warriors believing that help is not on the way for us. And as a result, we've become the Equalizers of our lives. Can I be honest? We begin to doubt our abilities, forgetting the promises of God. We tend to allow our eyes to shift from the left to the right, gazing while another flower blooms, wondering when that magical moment will happen for us. Not only that, but we grow weary in well doing, masking the behavior of a depressed drunkard asking our Creator the million-dollar question, "What about me?" You've decreed, and you've declared, you've waited, and you've smiled when you really wanted to cry and yes ma'am the other person's situation looked better than yours. Those days can become burdens, and those burdens aren't always light. One may diminish your trials and struggles to "This is life," but I, beloved, would like to think of it as destiny. For me, destiny is described as events that will happen to a particular person in the future.

Beloved, it's the "necessarily" that we take offense to. The flesh of us does not understand what's "necessary" but it's the Spirit man in you that will. There is a necessity for the good, the bad, and the ugly on this journey. Good days and bad days present themselves before and after God decrees a thing to you. They don't just come to frustrate you but to teach, guide and prepare. They become your roadmap to manifestation. It's your faith in the promise that will carry you through.

I walked away from the pulpit almost 10 years ago due to a sin that I willingly participated in for nearly 12 years. I lost my family, my home, and the friends we shared sided with him. Furthermore, I knew that I was wrong in what I was doing and as a result of private mayhem, I believed that I had forfeited the promises of God for my life. I watched other women in ministry grow exponentially, while I sat in dark rooms waiting for the enemy to consume my life. I believe that every bad thing to come was due unto me because of what I had done. Not only that, but I believe that the promises of God were null and void and that the anointing that I once possessed was of no effect. Like Hannah, I would open my mouth, but nothing would come out. The tongue that was once known as a bone crusher in the word had now become tied and cleaved. I no longer knew how to cry loud and spare not. I had settled in myself that God had forgotten about me. Yet, I had made peace with the thought of ever becoming someone great in the kingdom. Likewise, I had reconciled that my time had come and gone and that my popularity was over. I had settled that my womb was now closed. I believed and excepted the fact that there was possibly know latter rain for me.

Beloved, it is easy to go from belief to doubt when the necessity of what you have to go through for destiny doesn't appear to be working in your favor. When there is no evidence that God has his hands on your situation, not realizing that his timing is not your timing; it is not until we lose complete hope sometimes that God will send a messenger to remind us that He is faithful to finish what He started. My sister, I write to you today from a redeemed place to encourage you that God is incapable of forgetting you. He possesses all the ability and desire to strengthen you and to place you back in the race. Follow the directions on your journey, adhere to the speed limits, and remember that no matter how fast you go, the destination is still there. GO BACK and read the prophecies that were spoken. Believe and know that the anxiousness that you're about to experience is God stirring and moving in your heart. Rid yourself of unnecessary things for a rapid shift of advancement. Above all else, continue Your journey in His grace. You are and shall be forever remembered.

Verse to ponder: 1 Samuel 1:19

Minister Matokia Brown is a dedicated mother and nurse. She is a 1996 graduate of North Carolina Agricultural and Technical State University and a proud member of Alpha Kappa Alpha Sorority Inc. She is the mother of three amazing gifts, Christian, Taylor and Braxton. She grew up in a very protected family governed by her maternal grandparents.

The inspirations in her life and tragic death of her mother led her to establish a platform supporting women. Her first book is entitled "Ordained Sin." Discover more about this phenomenal and transparent woman by connecting with her on Facebook.

CRUMBS, THE REMIX

Dr. Grace Newell

Let me share a story or testimony with you; I met this guy, at a very young age. We grew together and became inseparable. He was so heaven-sent, I felt so blessed because in my mind I played my cards right, or so I thought. Nothing was going to stop this. We were going to become the definition of High School sweethearts. One night I was in bed and the Most High said "It's over" and here's why.

In the beginning, I was walking on clouds. We had a rough patch beforehand, but that is what happens to newer couples because in that stage you're still learning about each other. During this time, he was agnostic, and I, a believer. So, I introduced him to the family ministry, and surprisingly, he converted. It made me so happy because I knew ministry is going to be in my future and I couldn't have a spouse who would allow their confusion to fight with the gifting in me.

Years go by and we became heavy parts of the ministry. As I was in the building setting up chairs, praise dancing, and speaking behind the pulpit, my heart wasn't there. But it didn't matter to me, at that time, because I was too busy making sure his heart was. I was more worried about if he was reading the bible and praying that I wasn't even doing it myself, eventually, I was more worried about the next time I'd get to hear his voice or read his text than I was seeking the face of the Most-High to hear the voice of wisdom. My mind was so consumed with this guy that I thought "the Most-High could wait for me".

As my knowledge about this guy grew so did my love for him. I always wanted to hold him tight and keep him near. Because of this, I started to worry even more. I knew I had fallen too deep. I remembered my mother preaching about how if we put others before the Most-High, he'd remove them from our lives to prove there would be no other before him. Because of this I'd tell myself *"Do this for the Most-High so he won't take him away from you,"* and at the time I thought this was okay, forcing myself to do the bare minimum for the Most-High because I wanted to keep some guy in my life, not because I wanted to deepen my relationship with the Most High.

I was too in love to see the error in my ways. At the time, this guy and I were doing good, I thought I was doing something right concerning the Most-High. But after a while, I started to notice little things, he was taking wise counsel from the wrong people and when his friends spoke ill on my name, I was the one who had to defend me. When I brought it to his attention he apologized and promised to do better, so, I believed him and moved on.

Time goes by and another problem pops up with the same people. This time he desired to spend more time with them than he did me. I was so upset; I was receiving crumbs while his friends were being served full-course meals of quality time that was supposed to be spent with me. I completely ignored the fact that I had spent a few minutes giving the Most High a distracted prayer because I couldn't stop thinking about what this guy was going to say to me, so I could feel better about his actions. After bringing it to his attention he eventually apologized, I forgave him and moved on.

We then graduated and it was the start of a new future together. We were going to separate colleges, but we wanted to stay together. During this time, I was so concerned about how I would accommodate my life to be with this guy that I was ignoring the path the Most-High set for me. Time got closer for me to leave, and he proposed. To some it was a rash idea, to me it was perfect timing, a good way to test our love and keep me safe from campus predators. Once I got to campus everything was grand, I came home every weekend to be present in the ministry and see my fiancé, and to my knowledge, everything was still good. after a while, because of COVID, everyone got sent home. I thought this was great, I wouldn't have to suffer from the loneliness of the distance anymore.

I came home and I'm the center of his attention. I understood that attention couldn't last forever because he had stuff on his plate too, but just being on his mind filled me with joy. I was so understanding until I couldn't understand it anymore. Some days all I would get was a "good morning baby" I knew when he was working and when he was with his friends so I'd try to compromise "talk to me when you can, just let me know what's going on so I won't be worried all day" but after a while, I didn't even get that. I was so confused, he said he loved me so why was it so easy for him to treat me like an afterthought? Eventually, I brought it to his attention, and he apologized and promised he'd change. I forgave him but was still upset. I felt this way because I started to notice a pattern, change only lasted for a short time then we were back to square one.

Months went by and we were doing well so I was able to go to him whenever I was going through something and he was the first to say, *"How can I help?"* and if we had little disagreements, he was quick to apologize rather than turn everything around on me. In light of my happiness, the problems mentioned before were still present and getting worse, I just tried to ignore them because I wanted to be his peace. I wanted to prove to him he didn't make a mistake proposing to me and that he'd have a good life as my husband.

Eventually, I could no longer ignore the problems. I was tired of empty apologies and promises that would only be kept for a short time. So, I told him about himself, I wasn't taking it anymore. I waited for hours for him to read what I said and respond. As I waited, I prayed, for the first time in a while, and asked the Most-High to give him the words to speak if I had a future with him. After work, he finally read it. I was expecting him to apologize and tell me he was going to do better and work to be the man I deserve. I thought he was going to tell me what I wanted to hear because he was good at doing that. But this time was different, he told me if I was being treated so badly that he wanted me to leave and find better.

I was shocked; you don't just say stuff like that, so easily, to people you care about. However, I tried to shake it off, he'd just eventually apologize, and everything would be back to normal. But I couldn't let the actions that pushed me over the edge and the words that broke my heart go, not this time. The next day I laid in bed thinking about how hurt I was, then the Most-High spoke and told me "It's Over". After hours of fighting and thinking about the decision I was about to make, I finally listened to the Most-High and let go. Just like that, our relationship went from being, what I thought was unbreakable, to shattered pieces.

While reminiscing, I started to remember the disrespect I would let pass because I wouldn't want to start arguments. The wandering eyes with the confusing lies, the quick apologies to keep my emotions at bay, the dishonorable friends that got the protection from him that I deserved, and much more. Most importantly, I realized how I disrespected the Most-High while allowing myself to be treated this way. Here I was chasing after crumbs from some guy while the Most-High was calling for me ready to nourish me. I wasted years of my life worshiping the creation like it was the creator just to get knocked down when I was forced to realize he was just a guy and not a God.

Your age doesn't matter. Never allow a man, boy, etc., to become your Most High; these individuals do not know what path is best for you - they are the creation, not the Creator. People operate for their good, without the consideration of those around them. There is a sacred place only the Most-High should be able to abide. It's time to remove the people that have taken that space.

Dr. Grace or Prophetess Grace, is the youngest of five children, she is the daughter of Dr. Janet Patton-Newell and brother Derrick Newell. She was born in Pennsylvania but raised in North Carolina. Growing up all she knew was ministry, and being the child of a preacher, always expected to follow in those footsteps. She has had experience writing stories; this is her second publication. In the wake of whatever was thrown her way, she was taught the importance of keeping her faith, and knowing those situations will not be her end. Dr. Grace Newell holds multiple degrees and certifications, including a doctorate in Biblical Counseling. She assists her mother, Apostle/Dr. Janet Newell actively in ministry at Yeshiva Worship Worldspan/The Gathering at Yeshiva in Knightdale, NC. She can be contacted via Facebook.

MIRROR, MIRROR

Apostle Janet L. Newell

As a child, I didn't pay much attention to what society deemed as beautiful. As I grew older, I realized that self-perception is often dictated by how people view you. This led me from seeing 'just me' and being content to changing myself into someone else. Growing up, I could count on one hand how many times I heard my mom say, "You are beautiful." Reflecting back to the first time I heard her say those words was in my early teens. It was a profound moment for me because at that time I started developing strong insecurity. Standing over six feet tall, I was skinny and had major hair problems. What I noticed when I looked in the mirror was what I heard my peers say about me.

Occasionally, it was good, most times it was bad. Mostly boys bullied me and girls whom I realized had self-image issues themselves.

Later, I understood that I was a target for a generational curse called low self-esteem and low self-worth. My grandmother and mom both suffered from low self-esteem. Despite this, my mom did the best she could with raising two daughters in the midst of not having positive affirmation and encouragement from her mother. Honestly, I felt that I was the recipient of poor parenting by my grandmother.

Things began to happen to me as I began developing physically, things that were not natural; things that were not supposed to happen to a little girl. I was molested by extended family members. Raped by a neighbor and mishandled by those who, I thought, were the love of my life. These events led to more bondage that, as a young woman, I did not know how to overcome. I just maneuvered around them.

Fast-forward, I was a star athlete in my high school years and became an idol to many young and older than myself. Young girls wanted to be like me, and I was sought after by guys that were considered to be popular. Yet in all of that, I was having a hard time with my self-image.

I graduated and went to business school. Later, I quit school and joined the Army.

There were life-changing circumstances that took place in between, including giving birth to two beautiful children. First a beautiful little girl, then a handsome little boy. At the time, having body issues was not a problem. I'm saying this for a reason. Follow this journey with me as I describe why the body issues were not an issue after childbirth.

While in the military, I was sexually assaulted and harassed by men in my upper chain of command. This left me feeling like this type of behavior was just going to be a part of my life. As my life progressed and my career in the Army flourished, I became an overachiever. Excelling in everything, I also rose in rank, won competitions and became popular with many, even my chain of command. Additionally, I was a top athlete in the military and sought after by men from all walks of life. However, upon gazing into the mirror, I observed the insecure young girl who had been harmed mentally, emotionally, and spiritually by sexual, verbal, spiritual, and emotional abuse, as well as a period of physical abuse.

Everyone else saw a beautiful, confident and successful woman, but I saw my issues and flaws.

My life was a masquerade, and I wore a very convincing mask. I married and had two additional children. After my fourth child, I started experiencing body issues. I hit the gym. I ran myself into oblivion, working out to get that perfect body.

Needless to say, I married a man with image issues as well, and that marriage ended in divorce.

That is another book.

This husband was very abusive in many ways that were beyond my comprehension. This pushed me into a tailspin or a downward spiral inside, but on the outside I wore a smile and excelled tremendously.

Now when I looked in the mirror, I couldn't even see myself at all, just the monster that my ex-husband had created via his extreme abuse.

To my recollection, Yahuah was in my life all of my life, I just did not know nor recognize His voice or presence at the time. When I was pregnant with my firstborn, I was baptized, then received the Ruach HaKadesh (Holy Spirit) shortly after she was born. All of this happened before my second child was born. Not long after, I was placed in leadership and excelled in the Church. No one counseled me, nor did anyone walk me through my issues. My leaders saw the grace and anointing in my life. They were compelled by the gifting and used me up! All the while, I was struggling with fear and torment.

After working in the healing and deliverance ministry, I realized how desperately I needed healing and deliverance. My Yah! Yes, Yah used me for His glory, but I was like clay marred in the Potter's Hand. Yes, that was me right there. When I left my then husband, I returned to the same leadership. Only then I realized that I was being bullied, tormented and spiritually abused by them. They were like spiritual vampires to me, sucking all the life out of me; altering my identity, just as I allowed others to do in the past.

Once again, I excelled in the midst of my oppression. I developed programs, hosted successful gatherings, and did great outreach ministries. I moved in the gift of healing and miracles, preached the best under the table, and I loved Yah. Despite this, I spent my nights weeping. I loved my oppressive leadership and would have taken a bullet for them. I was unaware that I had Stockholm's Syndrome; I married once again to a young man that I had invited to fellowship with our congregation. He watched me in ministry and fell in love with me. He was a wonderful, loving man with more issues than I had. Furthermore, he supported me in all that I did in ministry. Before marrying him, I had concerns. I went to my Pastor for counseling and was made to feel like my concerns were invalid. I allowed myself to be pursued because I trusted his relationship with Yah more than mine.

Once again, in my brokenness, I married another broken man. By this time, I had four children and shortly after getting married, became pregnant with my fifth. Tragedy struck my home with the sudden death of my oldest son, Kellen. I felt hopeless, like I was created just to suffer and hurt. But through it all I held on to Yah's unchanging hand, so I thought. I dove into ministry and became super overprotective of my family. I stayed in the Word of Yah. Fasted and prayed until the cows came home; traveled, preached and saw the deliverance of many, but lived a personal horror story. This marriage ended with me leaving him and moving to North Carolina.

Now, when I looked in the mirror, I saw an abused woman with two failed marriages and a mourning mother who was abandoned by those who she relied and depended on. I saw a trapped woman who was stuck in a job where I was feeling overworked. Additionally, I saw a mother of five living in a city that did not have compassion for her situation. Not only that, I saw shattered pieces.

Even with all of this going on, I had morals and standards. I made a point to live in a way that my daughters and son would know that I did not and would not compromise my integrity.

Working on my education, I gained multiple degrees, certifications, and diplomas. Likewise, I quickly received a promotion to management. All while continuing in ministry: a typical overachiever activity. It was only when I heard Yah say, "When water goes through a pipe to refresh those who drink it, even the pipe gets wet," did I go through the most profound deliverance in my life." That continues to progressively work effectually in me. Yah was letting me know that the same anointing that destroys the yoke of bondage on the lives of the people that I minister to has the same yoke destroying power concerning my life. I'll say this, as I went throughout my life, I did walk out multiple deliverances and breakthroughs as I grew in Yah. But it was mind-altering and transforming when I came into the knowledge of my Hebrew heritage and the true power and purpose of the relationship that I had with my Creator. I began discovering the purpose of my existence, the benefits of the Holy Spirit dwelling within and the anointing in my life concerning my life in the year of Yah, 2005. Many major healings and deliverance began to occur quickly. Furthermore, I became aware of the many natural and spiritual blessings that I had acquired along the way.

My entire mindset immediately changed from being a victim to being victorious.

Many scriptures got me through the dark places. Many times I felt like I wasn't going to make it, and I am very sure that those of you who are reading this can relate to those places in your life. But I'm still here, not just here, but here with a testimony of Victory over what was supposed to kill me. I spent many times just saying, "I trust You," quoting Proverbs 3:5-6, *"Trust in Yah with all thine heart and lean not unto your own understanding, but in all of your ways acknowledge Him, and He will direct your path."* I would remind myself that I was fearfully and wonderfully made (Psalms 139:14). Rehearsing in my mind, "No weapon formed against me shall prosper (Isaiah 54:17) and I shall not die but live and declare the works of the Most-High (Psalms 118:17).

Beloved, the Word become my medicine, and I ingested the Word like a prescription. It was the Truths in The Word of Yah that set or made me free. The application of the Word of Yah was not a fairy tale or something that just works for someone else; the increased faith in my life for me and not just for those I prayed for. This was truly a faith journey; forgiving myself for things that I blamed myself for and was ashamed of that were not my fault and those that were my fault. HalleluYAH! Truly understanding what the Grace Of Yah was and how that Grace operated in my life. My mind was constantly reflecting on where I was in relation to myself, and so much more was revealed to me. Knowing beyond a shadow of a doubt that all things work together for good to those who love Yah, to those who are the called according to His purpose (Romans 8:28).

The cycle stops with me and my children. My children have been affirmed by me. I make sure that I encourage and nurture them. Furthermore, I speak to their self-worth, self-esteem, confidence, and perception of themselves as well; the same is done for my spiritual children and those that I mentor.

So let me tell you what the Mirror is saying when I look at it today. Today, I see a Daughter of Zion who has overcome tremendous obstacles with strength now to go back to the trenches to bring others out; a woman who has been in the fiery furnace, who was not burned or singed, but purified. One who was buffeted by the enemy ONLY to be polished and fine-tuned by Yah. Now, I am healed, delivered and set free.

The beauty of holiness and the Glory of Yah is in my life. I see the Fearful and Wonderful work of Yah. Furthermore, I chose to share this part of my life because I want you to know if Yah did it for me, He can do it for you. In my place of wholeness, I have drawn people of like mind and healing into my circle. The Scripture says encourage others with the words that you were encouraged with. I pray that as you read this and look in your ever present mirror that you will not just see the issues or flaws, but you will see the dawning of the restored, renewed and healed you!

Mirror, Mirror on the Wall

Dr. / Apostle Janet Newell, has traveled internationally and nationally preaching the unadulterated word of The Most High. Her earnest desire is for the people of Yah to be fully aware of who He is inside of them and in this earth. She is a Well Respected Leader, Elder, Morah and Mother in the Hebrew Community.

Apostle Janet L. Newell is currently the Founder and Overseer of Gathering At Yeshiva Worship and Prelate of Yeshiva Worship International Fellowship (YWIF) both of Knightdale, North Carolina. She is the President of YWIF School of Ministry and School of Prophets that was established in 2013. She is the Chancellor of Rehoboth International Bible College located in Knightdale, NC. RIBC is a Primarily Distant Learning and Correspondence Bible College as well as a Classroom College when need be.

In 2001 she was Affirmed an Apostle and 2003 Apostle Janet L. Newell planted Wind in the Word Outreach Ministries later named Wind in the Word Worship Center in Farrell, PA.

She received the honor of being listed in Marquis Who's Who among American Women 25th Silver Anniversary Edition for the year of 2006 and Marquis Who's Who among the World. Apostle continues to host many conferences, seminars and workshops believing that the application of practical Teaching of The Word of Most High is the key to a successful and victorious living.

She firmly believes education is paramount and has led by example. She holds a Diploma in Biblical Studies as well as an Honorary Doctorate of Humanities, which was conferred upon her in 2005 and an Honorary Doctorate in Christian Life Counseling in 2015. She has also achieved a Master Degree in Christian Counseling, Summa Cum Laude and a Bachelor Degree in Church Administration, Magna Cum Laude in 2010. All from New Covenant International Bible College of Decatur, Alabama. She earned her PHD in biblical Counseling, Diploma in Family Mental Health, Certificate in Marriage Counseling from Rehoboth International Bible College. She is also Certified in Creation Therapy (Arno Profile System) from Sarasota Academy of Christian Counseling and later became an International Representative which enabled her to certify others in Creation Therapy.

Apostle Newell has been seated on the Executive Board of New Covenant International Bible College and School of Prophets of Columbia South Carolina, Veronica Johnson Ministries of Las Vegas Nevada. She was also listed as an Adjunct Professor at Christ Restoration Institute and Seminary.

In 2015 Dr. Janet L. Newell assumed the position of Chancellor of Rehoboth International Bible College of Raleigh NC.

She has hosted a weekly Christian Radio Broadcast on *Kingdom Faith and Power Broadcast* called *Really Real Talk* and *Fresh Oil with Dr. Janet L Newell* on *The People's Channel*. She currently hosts *She Is Gathering* on *Winning In Prayer TV* located on Roku TV every Friday Night at 8:00 pm.

Dr. Janet L. Newell has ministered via radio, television and is a published author. Her most recent projects are: *My Little Prophet's Manual* and *Life's Paths* which can be purchased on Amazon.com. She has also contributed to other book projects and written forewords for best sellers. She was also published several times in *Fresh Oil Magazine*.

After all is said and done, Apostle Janet L Newell is a Servant to Most High's People and walks in Sonship pertaining to relationship with Most High.

Dr. / Apostle Newell can be reached via www.gatheringatyeshivaworship.org, via FB: DrJanet Newell and LinkedIn: She is Gathering

WINNING AT WEALTH

Lady Dana Branham

It sounds cliché but it is true… if I had a dollar for every time I have heard "They didn't teach us this in school" or "I wish they had taught us this in school," or "Why didn't they teach us this in school?" I might not be rich, but I would be sitting pretty with a little stash of cash on the side. I know it all to well myself, because I have two finance degrees and still did not learn the basics of personal finance that I should have. And if I did not learn it, I know others didn't. And it is a shame.

So, Sis, I am here to here to help you out. The money mess I found myself in was unfortunate to experience but has become the foundation upon which I can bless others with information and tips to know better so that they can do better. Whether you are in a money mess, trying to avoid one, or just want to learn more, the basics that we all missed out on are in my book. However, the following are my top five tips on what you need to know now to make your later greater... Hallelujah!

- **Don't let anyone else know more about your money than you – including your spouse or significant other!**

Sis, you do not have to be an expert, but you should know the basics enough to know if something is wrong. It's amazing that still in this day and age, at this age and stage, there are still some who let another control ALL of the household finances. Even if that is not your strongest point, knowing what is going on with your money is key to winning at wealth.

Even if you don't pay the bills, have a monthly meeting to discuss them and any plans you have for your money jointly or individually. Setting aside the time and the intention of understanding goes a long way to making wise decisions that will pay off down the road. Be proactive, rather than reactive, but most of all, be active as a participant in your household's finances.

- **Control some of your money!**

Even if you are a professional mom, find a way to earn some money to save for things that you want, places you want to go, and for your own future. Having control over at least some of your money is a level of freedom and security that most of us need for long-term peace of mind.

How do you choose what that is? Take an assessment of what you already know how to do, what you are good at doing, and what you love to do and research if there are ways to monetize one or all of them. For example, if you are a teacher, you might tutor on the side; or if you are an IT professional from 9-5, you might teach classes to senior adults at night. There are a myriad of options out there, surely there is one that will work for you.

- **If you are age 50 or older, make catch up contributions in your retirement accounts!**

Retirement income has changed, such that more and more, we must rely on our personal savings to get us through. Pensions have gone by the wayside and Social Security has been delayed for many of us. As a result, this option is significant because if you are like me, you have some money messes to make up for!

In your 401K or equivalent Employer-Sponsored Plan, you can save an additional $1,000 per year. That may not sound like a lot, but [hypothetically] if you save that $1,000 each year for 20 years and earn 8%, at the end of the 20 years, you will have $45,761.96. That could be a new car, a few extra vacations, some upgrades to your house, and more! I don't know about you, but I'll take it!

- **Insure everybody!**

Life insurance is the foundation of any good financial plan. It takes care of your business when you cannot. I know you do not want to leave any work undone, so please do the following:

Insure Your Children – To secure the coverage and to set them up for future success. This can be controversial but there is value in insuring your children while they are insurable and young. Premiums are based on age; therefore, you can pay less to insure them now than they would pay to insure themselves later. Insure them because we know that unfortunate things happen, but also to start building cash value up to use later to meet their financial needs.

Insure Yourself – To take care of your children or to take care of the business you want to support (i.e. donations to causes, gifts to charities, etc.) when you are no longer here. I have seen lots of financial plans where there is $1M on the husband, $100K on wife because she doesn't work outside the home. Don't shortchange yourself, the impact that you make in the world, and the chasm that will be left without you.

Insure your S.O. – To take care of you!! Even if you must pay for it yourself, *take care of you, Boo!*

- **Teach your children**

    Sister, please, please, please, teach your children or other little people in your life about money management. The school still might not get it right. We are still fighting for a formal financial literacy program in all schools, at all levels; and even when it is implemented, you will have to teach, reteach, and reinforce the lessons yourself. Not only because it is critical to their success, but so that you don't have to use your own savings to take care of them when they don't know!

    I pray that these tips will help you transform your financial life. There is much more to learn and do outside of these five things, but these are foundational and a set up to win at wealth. Blessings to you, Sister, on this journey. You can and will win at wealth and I cannot wait to witness your success!

Lady Dana S. Branham is a Certified Financial Planner™ and has worked in financial services for over 15 years. In 2018, she sold her advising practice to return to Corporate America, and now works at LPL Financial as a Vice President in the Business Transitions Division. Prior to becoming an advisor, she worked at a Union, in Construction, and at Lexmark International.

Dana is a graduate of Howard University, where she earned a Bachelor's of Business Administration degree in Finance and the University of Kentucky, where she earned a MBA. In addition to the CFP designation, she also holds several securities and insurance licenses and certificates.

Dana enjoys educating the community through seminars, workshops, and appearances. In 2019, she published her first book, *Money Mayday: 7 Steps to Cleaning Up Your Money Mess*, which walks readers through, in an easy conversational tone, the sometimes-difficult steps to cleaning up their money mess. Through a biblically based approach, Branham shares her own journey of cleaning up the mess created while operating her own business.

She is also the author of: "Winning at Wealth."

"My Daily Goal – Live in such a way, that people do not have to 'squint' to see the God-ness in you."

~ Lady Danielle Y. Miller

BONUS STUFF & INSPIRATION

Sister, I Understand ...

Remembering to respond with love instead of anger. In our understanding, when someone we love leaves us. A family member turns their back on you; at a time when you need them the most. Your best friend of 15 years decides to walk away from the friendship with no explanation. There will be times when life will not go your way. It will feel like everything you thought you knew about life won't feel familiar.

If we take a moment to step back, take the focus off ourselves to fully let responding with love be the action. Understanding that people react and say things out of their experiences and past trauma. Maybe a parent or someone they depended on really let them down. Perhaps even abandoned them because that was what was done to them by their parents or someone they highly regarded. Behavior is taught most times indirectly, and quickly becomes a way a person handles situations that cause others harm. They may reject you by leaving first so they don't experience that same pain again to them. Thinking well, I will leave them first, so it won't happen to me.

At first, you may not be able to respond to what happened to you right away. It may be best not too. This will give you some time to think about what was done or said and be able to process what happened. When you have had time to think about the other person's actions, you may still not want to communicate with them. You may decide to let them know how it made you feel. As well as asking them, "did someone do something to you in your past to hurt you?". Giving them an opportunity to introspectively look at themselves. It could be they never knew how to process their feelings if they were abandoned, rejected in previous relationships. It gives them a chance to break the cycle of repeating the behavior if they can see well my mom or dad acted this way. I was disrespected by a family member. The love I was shown was through shouting and being strictly disciplined.

God wants us to treat others by being kind, compassionate, and forgiving. If we take this approach when people mishandle us; it can help us show grace in the time, it's most needed.

Submitted by Ms. Shaffron Bey

"Situations and circumstances happen in your life for a reason; you're either going to let them tear you down or build you up - your response will determine your outcome."

~ Lady Debra Mack

- Self-awareness to me is acknowledging and dealing with my own insecurities, inadequacies and biases.

- Love is a gift not an obligation.

- Sometimes hurt looks like anger.

- Self-care, because you can't give from an empty cup.

Submitted by
Sonja T. Lane, School Counselor & Dream Coach

"God provides the canvas in which to paint our life's journey." ~Allison M. Kincaid

The beauty of art is thought to be held in the eye of the beholder but the true beauty is in the soul of the creator. Art therapy can utilize both relaxation of the mind and cleansing of the soul. This tool has been used in addiction settings to help extract and heal wounds by allowing the creative process to bloom through the use of non-verbal communication. This non-verbal communication acts as a gateway to healing. This form of therapy puts words to silence, and verbiage to the unspoken, opening a portal to healing.

Several years ago, I was working with a client who was in addiction recovery. The client had such a tragic past that haunting memories had been buried deep within the subconscious. It took one special art therapy directive that allowed years of suppressed emotions to emerge onto a canvas for the healing process to begin. It was through this client's participation and will to change that aided in the unlocking of memories. This pivotal moment allowed the client to express emotions through art before exploring their words. What a powerful moment. Had it not been for the power of Art Therapy healing may not come to fruition and this individual's life may not have changed.

It is through Art Therapy that this dynamic tool can allow the subconscious to reveal hurt and tragedy of the past in order to heal and create a new vision for the future. The use of color, texture, line and shape lay the groundwork for healing to begin. Talent is not necessary to utilize this amazing tool for it is the raw imagery that forms the words on the page.

Allison Kincaid *is an artist, art teacher/therapist and addiction counselor in Virginia and The Outer Banks, NC. She merges her knowledge of art and addiction to assist youth and adults through the healing process.*

"Be the intervention, not the crisis."

You don't have to retaliate every time shots are fired! It's ok to retreat and take cover. As humans, we're wired to listen to respond instead of listening to understand. Take time to process the exchange and ask yourself, what is the true motivation behind the exchange? Hit the pause button and consider the recourse of your reply. Is it something that might create further discord? Will it ruin a friendship or get you fired? How far could this escalate? The old saying is to take the high road, and taking the high road doesn't mean you're weak. The real flex is having the strength and self-control not to imitate the behavior. In doing so, you are intervening the situation, becoming the mentor instead of the opponent.

~ Rashae H. Brown, Director of Athletics

HOME BUYING TIPS

• Determine your budget and start saving for a down payment.

Pro Tip: You don't need 20% down, to purchase a property. If you are going to reside in the property it could be 3% - 5%. This is something you need to speak with a qualified lender to guide you to works best for you.

• Make sure your credit score is good. If not, work on improving it. A "good" credit score to buy a home typically is 660 or above. Again, please talk with a qualified mortgage lender to find out what they require. We have a wonderful trusted lender that is a good resource.

• Start researching neighborhoods to get an idea of where you want to buy.

• Get Pre-Approved so you know exactly what your budget is. This is your golden ticket! Once you have this you can start looking at homes.

• Find a trusted real estate agent we are always here to help, serve + guide you through the process and make sure you're protected and getting the best deal possible.

Krista + Mike Reed
REAL ESTATE BROKERS
MEGA ICON TEAM
TEAM LEADER
PREMIERE Group of eXp Realty

Krista and her husband are accomplished real estate brokers in the Inner/Outer Banks of NC.

reedteam@obxislandlife.com
252-216-2659
obxislandlife.com

RECIPES

Krista Reed's version of **PF Chang's Lettuce Wraps**

INGREDIENTS
- 1 tablespoon olive oil
- 1 pound ground chicken
- 2 cloves garlic, *minced*
- 1 onion, *diced*
- ¼ cup hoisin sauce
- 2 tablespoons soy sauce
- 1 tablespoon rice wine vinegar
- 1 tablespoon freshly grated ginger
- 1 tablespoon Sriracha, *optional*
- 1 (8-ounce) can whole water chestnuts, *drained and diced*
- 2 green onions, *thinly sliced*
- Kosher salt and freshly ground black pepper, *to taste*
- 1 head of romaine lettuce

INSTRUCTIONS
- Heat olive oil in a large cast iron skillet over medium high heat. Add ground chicken and cook until browned, about 3-5 minutes, making sure to crumble the chicken as it cooks; drain excess fat.
- Stir in garlic, onion, hoisin sauce, soy sauce, rice wine vinegar, ginger and Sriracha until onions have become translucent, about 1-2 minutes.

Stir in chestnuts and green onions until tender, about 1-2 minutes; season with salt and pepper, to taste.

To serve, spoon several tablespoons of the chicken mixture into the center of a lettuce leaf, taco-style.

LaSonja Lane's Vegan Pintos

Ingredients
- 2 lbs dry pinto beans
- 2 - 32 oz boxes vegetable broth
- 1 yellow or white onion (*chopped*)
- 1/2 red and/or green pepper (*chopped*)
- 4-6 Garlic cloves (*chopped*)
- Garlic powder
- Onion powder
- Bay leaves
- Baking powder (*pinch*)
- Black pepper (*I use course*)
- Celery salt or Himalayan pink salt
- Oregano (optional)
- Cayenne pepper (*optional*)

Other options: Add chopped portobello mushrooms, crushed tomatoes and/or vegan sausage

When using a slow cooker/crockpot or pressure cooker... Place broth and dry ingredients in pot together. I use this opportunity to taste test in case I want to adjust any seasonings. Add chopped onion, green/red pepper and garlic. You may prefer to sauté first; I don't. Add beans, stir, cook.

**For me...If using pressure cooker, set timer for ~ 35-40 minutes. Beans should be between slightly firm and falling apart in pot. Enjoy!

"Love many, trust few, learn to paddle your own canoe."

~ The Late Helen S. Mahoney
Nurse & Civil Rights Activist – Greensboro, NC

THE CONCLUSION OF IT ALL

Dr. Angel Miller (Angel Barrino)

In the following paragraphs, I expound upon the historical development of this project and I also address a few topics that are important for women to understand - ones that have not been addressed fully in previous chapters of this book. In this section, are some lessons I've learned and some tips to hopefully make your lives better as you navigate through your own journeys. ~ Dr. A

As aforementioned in the Introduction, when the idea of My Sister's Keeper was birthed, I wanted the book to be more like a coffee table publication inundated with originality – quotations, recipes, tips and tidbits of wisdom penned by women from all walks of life. That was the original design and concept for the book. However, it has evolved into an anthology of testimonies, emotional support, and more. My thought process began as such, *"I've compiled anthologies of this sort. I want something different."* Despite my desires, the book has taken a new trajectory and initially I found myself working through the acceptance of this new direction. In my head I knew exactly what I wanted, though I could not seem to articulate it effectively. The long journey of working on this book discouraged me from creating or developing future compilations. Nonetheless, Yah is still faithful.

Being a therapist in the fields of addiction recovery and trauma taught me several things as I prepared for the finalization of this project – the main concepts being acceptance and tolerance. Fully accepting my limitations with this book, I knew I had to press forward due to the commitment made to each contributing author. The main limitation was deciding what I wanted to share with my audience, and how transparent I needed to be regarding what I endured as I compiled this project.

Honestly, I wanted to scrap the entire project because I felt as if I did not have the capacity to forge ahead after losing my grandmother in 2021, and then losing several family members in 2023, not to mention the chaotic marital issues I was processing through. What is most important for my readers to know? These questions have resonated in my mind for approximately 2.5 years. Is it possible for me to be vulnerable as a leader, therapist, minister, and women's empowerment coach without putting my husband's foolery on "front street?" Continually, I would ask myself, *"Angel how can you best present an influential and powerful message to women without destroying your husband's character?"*

The past four years have been insane, to say the least … Excruciatingly painful emotionally and humiliating. Abandonment. Neglect. Disappearing Acts. Dishonesty. Infidelity. Chaos. Trauma and Anxiety ... the disrespect and dishonor to me and my family was unfathomable. Yet, still I rise. Despite his behavior, I have accepted accountability for not asking my husband the right questions and ensuring that he was Yah's best choice for me."

Fast forward... the icing on the cake was this past year. In May 2023, my "husband" was rescued from a five-alarm fire that left me incredibly emotionally distraught and feeling isolated. He REFUSED to include me or allow me to be part of this experience. The day before the fire, he messaged me saying he wanted to reconcile and that he wanted his wife back. The days and weeks that followed, however, were riddled with silence. Every day questions flooded my thoughts regarding whether he was okay. When I finally spoke with him, he said, *"I don't want to talk. Please take your post down from the fire department's page."* Periodically he would text and provide a glimmer of hope but then go silent again. Though he was acknowledged and celebrated for many heroic acts of courage and bravery displayed on that tragic day (by attempting to save lives), his overall actions and treatment toward me left me feeling further abandoned and neglected, having to process those traumatic events alone. He was not a "hero" in our marriage and relationship. But if I am honest, he was never a hero to me. He abandoned me long before this fire occurred. For many weeks, I found myself struggling with my feelings of being proud of him; yet angry with him simultaneously. Heartbroken by seeing this repetitively discussed on National News, yet, not knowing where he was or how he was doing, angered me more. As of publishing this book, I had not heard from him in several months. *Talk about acceptance...* the man who swore to provide and take care of me in the sight of God and other witnesses, bailed on me time and time again. Despite the historical occurrences of his abandonment track record, I decided to give him "one last chance," then he almost lost his life in a fire, and I barely hear from him again… to now, complete and total silence. Until recently, I didn't know whether he was alive. For a while, I stopped checking for him. Have I stopped loving him? Not really, but *"What's love got to do with it?"* This man deliberately participated in actions and behaviors which left me handling life without him. Listen Sis… *He showed me who he was. And I overlooked it.* Where does this leave me? Torn professionally. Why? Because daily I teach my clients to believe in themselves, build their worth and value – not based on anyone or anything but to focus on finding it within. The most powerful aspect of this experience is realizing that I had worked on myself emotionally enough over the past two years that I am handling this much better than expected. After all, I knew his character and integrity. Therefore, my resilience is much greater than it would have been over a decade ago. *Emotional work is difficult work.* I remind my clients of how difficult emotional work is at least two or three times per week.

Married, living single is a hard place but it is also a growth place. Years ago, I penned an article titled, *"Don't Die in the Valley;"* this was also my first sermon. Valleys are low places, but fertile places. Things grow in the valley. **Psalm 23:4 states, "Yeah though I walk through the valley of the shadow of death, I will fear no evil…"** Through this marital experience, I often found myself in the valley; however, I did not die there. Nor did I allow my husband's insanity and shenanigans to define me. The sting of it was so fresh that I could not speak about it. The shame and humiliation of it was ever before me and Yah continued to strengthen and cover me in the midst of it.

The Conclusion of it All

What are the lessons?

Lesson #1 Sis – the first moment you see the signs, understand that it is not your obligation to be his SAVIOR. My only regret now is that we did not resolve things in a peaceful way and I am still processing some anger associated with his dishonor toward me and my family.

Lesson #2 - Trauma begets trauma. My love was not enough to heal him. One catastrophic event after another happened in this marriage. His life had been plagued with unresolved trauma. Chaos followed him everywhere. Eventually, my eyes were wide open, and I realized it was in my best interest to distance myself before being destroyed.

Lesson #3 – When you belong to Yah, He will protect you from evil or all harm and danger. Now was my husband an evil person? I do not think he was evil, but he operated in a spirit that controlled his actions and mind state. He was harmful for me. He did not have my best interest. Over time, I saw glimpses of change or could hear a change in his voice. Unfortunately, by then it was too late. He resented me for relocating more than six hours away and I began to resent him for his lies and abandonment. Through my work as an addiction counselor, I teach wholeness and recovery. Applying this same teaching to my own life, my heart began the healing process. The treatment center I work for teaches recovery based on the 12 Step Fellowship of Alcoholics Anonymous (AA). We teach our clients that, "resentment is the number one offender," as outlined in the AA Big Book. Guess what beloved? I had to internalize this and begin demonstrating this concept as well.

Lesson #4 – Forgiveness is a process and the only one responsible for your healing is you; harboring resentments keeps you from moving forward. Do not let a man (or anyone) have that much power.

Marriage is an institution that should not be entered into without wise counsel. Though experts and lay people will attest that couples need to date for an extended period of time before marrying, I do not agree with this philosophy wholeheartedly. Based on the Word of Yah, which is a believer's playbook for life – I don't believe it takes forever for a couple to "tie the knot." However, I do understand that this process requires preparation and inquisition. Ask all the right questions, answer honestly to all questions and life can be a joyful journey together. This is what I believe. In my case, my husband's motives were abhorrently wrong. He did not mean well for me. His actions were selfish, self-centered, and potentially malicious based on the spirit of manipulation he was driven by. Beloved, if you find yourself in a similar circumstance, work toward acceptance. *"Acceptance is the answer for all my problems today.[i]"*

Thankfully, Yah protected me from the worst of my husband's actions. Without shadow of doubt, I believe that the angels of Yah have been encamped around me and nearly every disruption has been blocked. When I say that Psalm 91 has been evident in my life over the past three years – whew!

Lesson #5 Sis – Even if your marriage fails, continue praying for your husband. Pray for him to walk into his purpose or destiny, even if his future does not include you.

My sharing these lessons with you is from my experience and lessons learned before, during, and after my marriages. Am I an expert on healthy marriage? No! Am I knowledgeable of Yah's Word concerning healthy marriage? Yes! My grandma Louise was the epitome of strength & dignity. She remained married to my granddaddy Paul until death separated them. That was 50 years! This woman understood the assignment of COVERING and being a wise woman, prudent wife. She was direct, yet her words were seasoned with grace and honey. But did she mean business? Yes, she did, and she handled her business concerning work, family, ministry.

As a child, I wanted a happy and healthy family. Sadly, I have not experienced that YET. However, I have a beautiful daughter from my first union, and if I knew then what I know now I might not have made so many mistakes back then. But I refuse to live with regret (or resentment) and as previously stated, regret and resentments will hinder you from healing.

Another lesson I learned in marriage is to NEVER leave the house while having an argument or disagreement. My married friend girls always told me, "Go to another room, but don't leave the house in anger." This resonated with me and is one of the most powerful lessons I've learned for relationships. Additionally, I learned to never go to bed angry with your spouse. This, of course, is easier said than done, especially if your spouse is stubborn. This is lesson #6 Sis. The bible teaches in Ephesians 4:26-27, "'In your anger do not sin" Do not let the sun go down while you are still angry, and do not give the devil a foothold.'" In His Word, Yah has an answer for every circumstance we experience.

This leads me to the deeper discussion of anger. Was I angry with myself, my husband, and others in my life? Of course. Anger is a healthy emotion when properly processed. However, addressing issues when angry can be detrimental for oneself and others. Through my journey of becoming a therapist, I learned healthy ways of processing my anger. Initially, over a decade ago, I attended an emotion regulation course, TWICE. The first time I quit. IT WAS TOO HARD! Now I teach clients that emotional work is hard work, but necessary and to heal one must go through it and process it appropriately.

Lesson #7 Sis – Don't be afraid to get the help you need. Cry, scream, write, or whatever you need to do to get through the anger. More importantly, seek Yah's counsel, and seek professional help if you need it. Sis, I was the poster child for ANGER MISMANAGEMENT ... now I teach others how to effectively express anger without damaging themselves or someone else.

Lesson #8 Sis – If your marriage or relationship does not survive, build yourself emotionally, spiritually, mentally, and physically so that you do not miss a beat after he leaves.

Always remember, "Love never fails. If it fails, it was not love." ~ DH Bonner

Lesson #9 – Single Sisters, do not give up, keep praying. If you want a companion, pray for yourself to be the woman Most High wants you to be. Work on yourself, stay focused on your purpose and place yourself in position to be found by someone who possesses God's heart toward you.

Lesson #10 – Sometimes you must realize that the only mistake you made was allowing him to get too close to you.

THE NEXT TWO TOPICS ARE GRIEF & TRAUMA

Grief, let's chat about it… How do we get through the process of experiencing grief and loss? One day at a time, with intention. The obvious cause of grief is a physical death of a loved one or close friend. All too often, my family and I have experienced this. I would say that from last June to September was the most difficult for my family. Back-to-back death was experienced. It seemed as if we had a death in our family every week. The grief was overwhelming. Normally, I process things very well. However, for a few weeks I felt numb. The pain was exhausting.

According to *Psychology Today*, "Grief is the acute pain that accompanies loss. Because it is a reflection of what we love, it can feel all-encompassing. Grief is not limited to the loss of people, but when it follows the loss of a loved one, it may be compounded by feelings of guilt and confusion, especially if the relationship was a difficult one.[ii]" Depending on the school of thought, there is five stages of grief or seven. As a counselor, I typically walk clients through five stages: denial, anger, bargaining, depression and acceptance. Firmly, I believe that individuals who do not process through these stages effectively remain *stuck* and live with unresolved turmoil. Due to the scope of this book, I don't want to explain each step but invite you to read the associated article; however, I want to share some strategies I've used to assist with the healing process: (1) Find a way to honor the person's life or legacy. This is especially important if the loss was tragic or unexpected. (2) Stay active, participate in activities or hobbies you enjoy, especially during the commemoration of the loss, special days, birthdays, etc. (3) Practice self-care, which includes crying or expression of emotions. (4) Write in a journal. (5) Think of healthy memories (6) Travel during difficult times or do something opposite of depressive feelings.

Loss is a normal part of life; therefore, grief is expected; however, it can be processed in a healthy manner. You may never get over the loss, but you can get through it.

My next concern for my sisters is unresolved traumatic experiences or PTSD. Many women (men and children) are living with trauma. But because women give birth to generations, I believe when the hearts, minds, and lives of women our men and children will also be healed. Studies show that a pregnant woman experiencing trauma can pass the trauma to her unborn baby. According to an article by Mayo Clinic, "Trauma is the leading cause of no obstetric death in expectant mothers, affecting 7 percent of all pregnancies; most often trauma occurs in the third trimester. Major trauma has been associated with 7 percent of maternal and 80 percent of fetal mortality.[iii]"

Working with trauma clients is one of my specialties. Trauma is relative to the individual and I teach clients that no one's traumatic experience should be diminished or treated as unimportant, though many individuals tend to compare; there really is no comparison. A traumatic experience can be a number of different sudden and acute, emotionally painful experiences. The American Psychological Association or APA defines trauma as "any disturbing experience that results in significant fear, helplessness, dissociation, confusion, or other disruptive feelings intense enough to have a long-lasting negative effect on a person's attitudes, behavior, and other aspects of functioning. Traumatic events include those caused by human behavior (e.g., rape, war, industrial accidents) as well as by nature (e.g., earthquakes) and often challenge an individual's view of the world as a just, safe, and predictable place.[iv]" Traumatic experiences can also be related to domestic violence, simple assaults (including sexual assaults or molestation that do not result in a rape), and other acute injuries or even fires.

A person experiencing multiple traumas is often diagnosed with PTSD or post-traumatic stress disorder or complex PTSD.

What about anxiety and depression? Millions of women are suffering from anxiety and depression. Women are historically marginalized and find themselves not being accepted equitably and fair across all marketplaces. With the added pressures to perform, parent, protect, and pursue women find themselves "stretched thin" and overwhelmed emotionally, physically, spiritually, and mentally. Addressing these issues is imperative, preferably without medications and harmful alternatives. Statistically, I believe more women are seeking healthy solutions today than in years past; however, many are still suffering silently. Recently, I read about the administrator of an HBCU committing death by suicide after reportedly providing the president of the college with details regarding her continued mental health challenges and experiences while working for the college. This incident is only one of many issues regarding the disparities that women face in high profile jobs. Imagine the heightened emotions of women who may not have such careers. Psychology Today and other mental health outlets provide in depth data regarding how many women suffer from anxiety and depression, or other severe mental health challenges. According to www.statista.com[v], 27.2 percent of women in the U.S. had some type of mental illness in 2021. For 2023, please refer to Mental Health America's data for mental health adult mental health information.[vi]

As a person in recovery from depression and anxiety, being a granddaughter of alcoholism, and having numerous family members who suffer from or have suffered from mental health concerns, I am passionate regarding helping women and others receive assistance. For this reason, I am grateful to be a founding member of the NAMI OBX board (National Alliance on Mental Illness). Supporting NAMI efforts, particularly in North Carolina is a tremendous honor and I look forward to continuing this work.

So beloved, how do we get through these adverse circumstances in life? If you're a believer in Yah and His Word, you get through them by reading his Word, praying, remaining steadfast and unmovable. However, I do realize that every woman reading this may not be a Hebrew, Christian or believer in Most High and that's okay. I believe Most High gave me the charge to make this book available for multiple markets. As a therapist in a secular and biblical world, I work with women (and men) from all walks of life and I am grateful for the opportunity to share experience, strength and hope with all. The following list of safety and self-care strategies are things I use for myself and provide to clients to help facilitate the healing process. My prayer is that you will develop a wellness routine that works for you. The list below is not exhaustive, and honestly some of these things I just started implementing in 2023, but they work.

Beloved Sisters thanks for supporting this project and sharing it with others

SAFETY AND SELF-CARE:

Walking

Reading

Listening to music (I choose this based on my mood)

Shelling

Volunteering

Networking

Drinking Herbal Tea or caramel hot chocolate (Coffee drinkers you can choose your favorite coffee/brew)

Spending time with dogs

Going to the movies

Bowling

Skee Ball or other arcade games

Spending time at the beach

Fellowshipping with other believers

Listening to podcasts/YouTube Videos

Shopping

Social Media Interactions

Meaningful work/employment

Eating at my favorite restaurants

Crafting

Visiting museums or other historical venues

Resting/Taking a nap

Pausing/Breathing

Grounding

Exercise/Fitness

Visiting art galleries

Grocery shopping

Vacations

Take care of your vehicle

Pedicures/Manicures

Always keep at least $20 in your bag or car.

Buy a nice piece of furniture or something else you enjoy.

Take a train ride.

Take a day trip to a place you've never visited.

Keep hand lotion/cream in your purse or car at all times.

Pay your bills.

Save money.

Invest

Get involved in your community.

Pause. Breathe. Relax.

Believe in yourself.

Replace negative thoughts with positive thoughts.

State positive affirmations.

Find new meaning and value.

ABOUT DR. ANGEL MILLER

Dr. Angel Miller (Formerly Angel Barrino) is a Substance Abuse & Trauma Counselor and works at Changing Tides Oceanfront Treatment Center in Kitty Hawk, NC. She is a native of Greensboro, NC, currently living in the Northern Outer Banks of NC, by way of Charlotte and Gastonia. She earned her Bachelors in Christian Education, Masters in Christian Counseling, Honorary Doctorate in Sacred Literature from Rehoboth International Bible College in Raleigh, NC. She holds multiple certifications in Mental Health Recovery, Trauma and other specialties. She is a Certified Alcohol and Drug Counselor (CADC, ICADC) with approximately 9 years of experience in the Mental Health and Substance Abuse field. Angel joined MH/SA after realizing that she wanted to help others who were affected by alcoholism and trauma, as much as she had been as a child. She helps clients focus on solutions and identify ways to improve their quality of life. Her own life experiences and ability relating to clients in ways which help bring positive breakthrough have been her strength. She has a unique ability to teach clients from a wholistic perspective and her passion for complete recovery shines through in each group or individual session. Angel has an extensive trauma background, which includes working with victims of Domestic Violence, Human Trafficking and Sexual Assault. She is an active member of NAMI OBX and works closely with NAMI and other agencies to speak about awareness, trauma and advocacy.

When Angel is not working, she enjoys writing, singing, creating, reading, working in ministry, traveling, walking, playing with her pups Angel2 and Remy Jr., spending time with her daughter, family and close friends, as well as exploring cultural activities and new restaurants. She blogs about her dining experiences and adventures. Angel is an 11-time Best Selling author on Amazon and owns a private counseling, consulting and coaching business. This book reached TOP 100 on Amazon during pre-order status.

In March 2023, Angel earned her PhD in Biblical Counseling and has recently launched a part-time faith-based practice in the Outer Banks and online. She can be reached via her website www.drangelmiller.com, IG: @drangelrmiller Facebook: @DrA and LinkedIn: www.linkedin.com/in/angel-barrino.

"Charm is deceptive and beauty fleeting, but a woman who fears Yah [the Lord] is to be praised."

~Proverbs 31:30

REFERENCES

i   Authorized *King James Bible*. (2003). Thomas Nelson, Inc. (Original work published 1769)

ii   Authorized *King James Bible*. (2003). Thomas Nelson, Inc. (Original work published 1769)

iii   Authorized *King James Bible*. (2003). Thomas Nelson, Inc. (Original work published 1769)

iv   NAS Exchaustive Concordance of the Bible with Hebrew-Armanic and Greek Dictionaries Copyright @1981, 1998 by The Lockman Foundation. Lockman.org (biblehub.org) s.v "Breathe"

v   Authorized *King James Bible*. (2003). Thomas Nelson, Inc. (Original work published 1769)

vi   NAS Exchaustive Concordance of the Bible with Hebrew-Armanic and GreekDictionariesCopyright @1981, 1998 by The Lockman Foundation. Lockman.org (biblehub.org) s.v "Breathe"

vii   Authorized *King James Bible*. (2003). Thomas Nelson, Inc. (Original work published 1769)

viii   Authorized *King James Bible*. (2003). Thomas Nelson, Inc. (Original work published 1769)

ix   Authorized *King James Bible*. (2003). Thomas Nelson, Inc. (Original work published 1769)

x   Hymn, *It Is Well With My Soul*, Song by Audrey Assad

i   Alcoholics Anonymous, page 417

ii   www.psychologytoday.com/us/basics/grief#the-process-of-grief.

iii   Trauma in pregnancy: A unique challenge - Mayo Clinic

iv   APA Dictionary of Psychology

v   www.statista.com

vi   The State of Mental Health in America 2023: Adult Prevalence and Access to Care - NextStep Solutions (nssbehavioralhealth.com)

www.ingramcontent.com/pod-product-compliance
Lightning Source LLC
Chambersburg PA
CBHW072008290426
44109CB00018B/2177